JB JOSSEY-BASS

Retiring the Generation Gap

How Employees Young and Old Can Find Common Ground

Jennifer J. Deal

BICENTENNIAL
1807
WILEY
2007
BICENTENNIAL

John Wiley & Sons, Inc.

Center for
Creative
Leadership
NORTH AMERICA EUROPE ASIA
www.ccl.org

Published by Jossey-Bass
A Wiley Imprint
989 Market Street, San Francisco, CA 94103-1741   www.josseybass.com

Readers should be aware that Internet Web sites offered as citations and/or sources for further information may have changed or disappeared between the time this was written and when it is read.

Jossey-Bass books and products are available through most bookstores. To contact Jossey-Bass directly call our Customer Care Department within the U.S. at 800-956-7739, outside the U.S. at 317-572-3986, or fax 317-572-4002.

Jossey-Bass also publishes its books in a variety of electronic formats. Some content that appears in print may not be available in electronic books.

Library of Congress Cataloging-in-Publication Data

Deal, Jennifer J.
   Retiring the generation gap : how employees young and old can find common ground/ by Jennifer Deal.
        p. cm.
   Includes bibliographical references and index.
   ISBN-13: 978-0-7879-8525-7
   ISBN-10: 0-7879-8525-2
  1. Work.   2. Conflict of generations.   3. Intergenerational relations.   4. Psychology, Industrial.   I. Title.
   HD4901.D38 2007
   650.1'3—dc22

                                                    2006028741

Printed in the United States of America
FIRST EDITION
HB Printing   10 9 8 7 6 5 4 3 2 1

A Joint Publication of
The Jossey-Bass
Business & Management Series
and
The Center for Creative Leadership

Contents

Preface

People often ask why I chose to study generational conflict; some even want to know whether I chose this topic because I harbor some deep-seated anger toward people of other generations. *Did you have conflicts with your parents when you were a teenager?* (Didn't every reasonably healthy adult?) *Did you have problems with authority figures, such as your Ph.D. adviser?* (No comment.) *Do you disrespect older people?* (No!)

Actually, I have been lucky to have had my life enriched by the influence of relatives from generations that are not included in this research because very, very few are still in the workplace and, sadly, most are no longer with us—the so-called "Lost Generation" (although none I have known seemed lost) and the World War II Generation (the "Greatest Generation"). I grew up with the example of my grandmother, who, when my grandfather died too young, took over and ran his roofing company, raised two children, wore a dress and nylons to work every day, lived with diabetes for forty years, and never *ever* complained about the hand that life dealt her. As she climbed ladders to inspect roofing jobs in the 1940s, 1950s, and 1960s, she may have become the model for the feminist saying, "As you climb the ladder of success, don't let the men look up your dress." My grandmother (who was born in 1903) and other older relatives always told me that age was immaterial—that attitude, dedication, and effort were much more important.

So, generational conflict wasn't my primary area of interest, at least not initially. I was finishing another project focused on what makes a good global manager, and was writing a book about the results with my colleagues (Dalton, Ernst, Deal, and Leslie, 2002) when another colleague suggested strongly (on the order of "Get your backside to this meeting!") that I come to a meeting about a new research project on intergenerational conflict. She thought I might be interested in getting involved. She pointed out that the project didn't have a full-time researcher on it yet and that my other project was ending soon. Why not, I thought; it never hurts to gather information.

When I arrived at the meeting, I wasn't convinced that this topic was worth much time, because I honestly didn't think the issue of generational similarities and differences was important. It certainly wasn't important in my life (at the time). I also thought that any generational conflict was relatively unimportant to clients and would be (research-wise) relatively uninteresting to study. But I emerged several hours later intrigued by the research, both because of how useful it would be for our clients and because of how interesting the questions were (I'll say more about this in the Introduction).

How different are the generations, really? How important is generational conflict in the workplace? What, if anything, can people in organizations do to reduce the conflicts among people of different generations? Contrary to my initial thoughts, the issues that were driving the research were both compelling and timely. For one thing, I learned that many of our clients at the Center for Creative Leadership believed that they had ongoing problems with generational conflict. For another, the published material on generational issues seemed to be too consistent with the stereotypes to be true. (Call me suspicious if you like, but when what is published on a topic echoes the stereotypes this closely, I suspect that people are just finding what they're looking for, rather than what is actually there.) Further, too little of what had been published relied on what I considered to be good, rigorous research for me to accept the conclusions. (Although the joke among social science researchers is "data is the plural of anecdote," basing conclusions on a small number of interviews isn't the sort of "data" I am comfortable relying on.) What was written was interesting, but I would never use it to make recommendations to a client.

It also seemed likely that demographic shifts projected by the Bureau of Labor Statistics to be coming (between 2005 and 2020) will have a much larger impact on the work world than the previously published material indicates they would. This meant that the information we hoped to discover through our research was going to be useful to clients immediately, was likely to be useful for at least a decade, and could potentially be useful for decades to come if we continued to gather data. That seemed to me to be a solid business case for the research project.

So we began the work. The more we learned, the more intrigued we became. The more interesting trends we discovered, the more we were able to tell clients about the *realities* of the differences and similarities among the generations. The more time we spent talking with clients about what we were finding, the more glad they were to tell us about what they were seeing in their work, which helped us focus our questions even more. This research project was supposed to take three years and has now been ongoing for seven. It is likely to continue for the foreseeable future as the next generation (Generation Y/Boomlet) moves into the workplace.

You'll see in the rest of this book the distillation of what we think are the most applicable and interesting results of the research. By necessity, the book doesn't contain everything. (Is anyone except my coworkers interested in 1,000 pages of minutiae, dozens of spreadsheets, and a plethora of chi-squares, Fs, Ts, and the other fun symbols that brighten a statistician's day?) What it does contain are the results of the research we hope will be most interesting and useful to people working in organizations that employ people from several generations—and that's almost everybody!

Why This Book Says "We"

You'll notice that I say "we" a lot, even though my name is the only one on the cover. The reason I do this is because I didn't do this work all by myself. Not even close. I was research scientist and project manager, but in truth, the research and the book itself were completed only because many people were willing to do a lot of work.

It's amazing to me how many people's work goes into the production of a book—or at least went into this one! In the past when I've read authors' notes saying, "This book couldn't have been written without the work of a number of people, yada, yada," I've always thought, "How gracious, but not necessarily true." I was really *really* wrong. Really. The number of people who were kind enough to spend their personal time commenting on my work rather than doing something important to them was incredible. It is a gift that I'll never be able to thank them for enough . . . and that I'm sure they'll be reminding me of forever . . . especially when it's time to pick up the check!

Seriously though, this book could not have been written without the efforts of an almost endless number of people, many of whom are listed in the acknowledgments.

Why We're Writing to Everyone and Not Just to Managers and Leaders

One question we wrestled with was whether this book should be written for people in positions of authority (managers, leaders, and the like) or aimed at a more general audience. Given that we are the Center for Creative Leadership, we began with a definite "leader" tilt. However, I think of generational conflict as an issue everyone experiences, not one that only people in positions of authority encounter. After all, everyone has parents, and many people have children—and through those relationships people experience the most volatile generational conflicts there are. So when I was writing I found that I was writing for everyone, not just for the people who have "VP" or "director" (or whatever) next to their name. After the editors read the first draft, we decided that we should make a conscious decision to go with the "everyone" orientation, rather than try to twist the whole thing back in the direction of people in executive positions.

So this book is written for everyone who has to interact with people from other generations (at work or at home) and occasionally finds himself or herself confused, annoyed, ticked off (or worse!) by the behavior of people of a different generation. And again, that is obviously . . . everyone!

However, people in management positions don't have to deal with generational conflict only as individual people; they also have to deal with other people's generational conflicts. Therefore, we've included special sections for those people who manage others (at any level) or who are anticipating moving into managerial positions.

A note on style: you've probably already noticed that I'm not writing in anything approaching a standard academic style. Rather than write with the (academically) obligatory dense prose, page-length sentences, and copious footnotes, I have opted for a more conversational tone. I hope for your sake that it makes the book easier to read!

September 2006
Jennifer J. Deal
San Diego, California

Do Not Pass Go Without Reading This Chapter!

Children today are tyrants.
They contradict their parents, gobble their food,
and tyrannize their teachers.
SOCRATES (470–399 B.C.)

If you read no further than this paragraph, we want you to leave knowing two things:

1. Fundamentally people want the same things, no matter what generation they are from.
2. You can work with (or manage) people from all generations effectively without becoming a contortionist, selling your soul on eBay, or pulling your hair out on a daily basis.

Got that? Good. You've got the essence of what we'll be talking about. Now (if you must) go check your e-mail, take a call, whatever. But then come back, because there's more to the story. . . .

"But what about the generation gap?" you may ask. "If you knew the old farts/young slackers (choose one—or more!) I work with, you'd know that the generation gap is alive and well!"

Well, appearances can be deceiving, whether it is gray hair and wrinkles, or jeans and pierced body parts. In fact, as we'll explain, the so-called generation gap is, in large part, the result of miscommunication and misunderstanding, fueled by common insecurities and the desire for clout—which includes control, power, authority, and position.

1

How We Got Here

This book introduces and explains a set of principles that come out of an extensive research project conducted by the Center for Creative Leadership (CCL) on managing and leading across generations. Why principles? Because they are the easiest and most intuitive way to explain thousands of results from our research. (We presume you don't *really* want to read through a 25-page spreadsheet that contains all the statistical results.)

But you should know that we were not in search of principles per se when we began our research. We were instead driven simply to explore the working world in search of answers to a number of questions our clients had asked, including these:

What do we need to do to retain younger employees?

Why is there so much conflict among the generations?

Why do older employees hate change so much?

What do younger people want to learn?

Do younger people want all development through their computers?

Why do younger people dress so informally at work?

What can we do about the feeling of entitlement among younger employees?

What can we do about the feeling of entitlement among older employees?

Why are younger people so disrespectful, and what can we do to fix the problem?

Why are younger people so disloyal?

Do older people have any interest in learning?

Why don't our employees trust us? Is it a generational thing?

Who wants coaching?

What do younger people want in their leaders?

As it turned out, the answers to these questions—and dozens more—can be effectively summed up by ten principles that apply across all generations. And, as the research revealed, dealing effectively with people of other generations can be pretty straightforward.

*In all matters of opinion and science . . . the difference
between men is . . . oftener found to lie in generals than in
particulars, and to be less in reality than in appearance.
An explanation of the terms commonly ends the controversy,
and the disputants are surprised to find that they had been
quarreling, while at the bottom they agreed in their judgement.*
—David Hume (1711–1766), *Essays Moral,
Political, and Literary,* 1875

So this book explains (when possible) what you can do to retire the generation gap and why you should. In each chapter, you'll find

- A description of the issue
- A description of our research on the issue
- The principal conclusion of the research expressed as a principle
- Our best take on how to apply the principle to make cross-generational work life easier for you

By the end you should know what your employees and colleagues at work are really saying when they cry "Generation gap!" and what you can do to "retire the gap" so you can address the real issues.

We don't promise that you're going to like everything we say—in fact we're sure that just about everyone is going to object to something in this book. But when we say things that offend you, please understand that it is not our intention to offend; we are simply trying to understand how one part of the world works, and good science sometimes leads to unexpected—and sometimes uncomfortable—conclusions.

About the Research

When you're reading about the conclusions of any research project, it is often difficult to know what you should believe and what you shouldn't.

There are three kinds of lies: lies, damned lies, and statistics.
—attributed by Mark Twain to Disraeli

Sometimes it is nearly impossible to tell when people are manipulating data to sell their theory (or their product or their political agenda). Therefore, we promise the following:

- Our results are as accurate as we can possibly make them; we aren't playing games with the statistics to support a particular position. If the data had shown that older people are fossilized and younger people are slackers, we would have reported that result.
- Our conclusions are drawn from our best understanding of the results as a whole. We aren't taking one result in isolation and building a whole theory around it.
- Our recommendations are based on our best understanding of the results and include knowledge gleaned from many other researchers, consultants, and organizational scientists.
- The quotations we use are entirely accurate and are drawn from our database. We have not altered the quotations for effect, though we have corrected spelling when the original was difficult to read.
- The stories we use are *all* true. We couldn't believe that people would actually do some of these things, but they did.

We also need to take some time to tell you about the people who participated in this survey, because they are not representative of everyone everywhere in the United States. Understanding who filled out the survey will help you understand how far you can generalize the results, so please bear with us for the next few pages.

As of the publication of this book, more than 5,800 people have participated in this research. Of that number, 3,200 who were both born in and are currently living in the United States were included in the research for this book. Those who either were born outside or are currently living outside the United States (the other 2,600) were not included because explaining every similarity and difference of generations for the rest of the world in addition to the United States would have made the book far too long. We may be using their data for another book in the future.

Although the database comprises 3,200 respondents, not every one of those individuals filled out every part of the survey. The results we report are based on the total number of people who responded to an item (not necessarily the total 3,200). For example, only 2,732 people responded to the question about retention, so those results are based on 2,732 respondents. Also, we didn't ask specific questions about change or respect in the workplace, so the results in the corresponding chapters are based on the comments of those people who volunteered information on those topics—a small subset of the total number of respondents. Nonetheless, we have reported only those results for which we believe we have ample evidence.

People began filling out the survey in 2000, and we stopped adding people to the database for this book in 2005. (An interesting aside: we have been unable to find any differences in responses between the people who filled out the survey before the events of September 11, 2001, and those who did so after.)

People who filled out the survey were born between 1925 and 1986. As of this writing, they are between the ages of 19 and 80. We assigned them (based on birth year) to a generation with this terminology and distribution:

Generation	Percentage of Survey Participants	Description
Silents (b. 1925–1945)	7.5	This group is called the Silent Generation because it tends to be quieter than the Baby Boomers and isn't discussed as much, but if you look at the organizations controlled by people in this age range, you will see how powerful the members of this generation are.
Early Boomers (b. 1946–1954)	27.9	These were the children born following World War II. There was a massive increase in the birth rate, known as the Baby Boom, that began shortly after the end of the war.
Late Boomers (b. 1955–1963)	29	This is the second half of the Baby Boom.
Early Xers (b. 1964–1976)	30.1	The group identified as Gen X began when the birth rate decreased after the end of the Baby Boom. The term *Generation X* became widespread

		after the publication in 1991 of Douglas Coupland's book of the same name. Coupland's book followed Charles Hamblett and Jane Deverson's 1964 novel, also titled *Generation X,* which described the generation of people who would come of age at the end of the 20th century as apathetic and materialistic.
Late Xers (b. 1977–1986)	5.5	This group includes the youngest part of Generation X.

People who filled out the survey came to us from a variety of places and types of companies, and they participated for a variety of reasons:

- Their organizations agreed to participate.
- They saw us speak about the subject and wanted to find out what was going on in the research.
- It was part of the work required before they came to a CCL program.
- They read about the research in a news article and wanted to put their two cents in.

We welcomed everyone who wanted to participate; all a person needed in order to become part of the research was a password from one of the research team, and we gave these out freely.

Of these 3,200 respondents, 41% were men, and 59% were women. Why so many women? Because we had a large sample from nonprofits, and more women worked in the nonprofits than worked in the for-profits. And no, there were no significant differences between for-profits and nonprofits regarding anything we'll be discussing.

Of the people who identified themselves by race, 88% self-identified as white, 6% as black, 1% as Asian, 2% as multiracial, and 3% as other. Why did we choose these categories instead of the ones that are used more commonly to describe race in the United States? Because we were conducting the study simultaneously on other continents, and we had to use racial categories that were as applicable in Timbuktu and Thailand as they were in Topeka; the racial categories generally used inside the United States are not commonly understood outside the country. Why were there so few nonwhites who participated? We have no concrete explanation, but we guess it is because the organizations that participated did not have a large percentage of nonwhites at the levels in the organization that participated. Where we were able to, we ran analyses looking for differences by race, but there weren't any of note.

Figures I.1, I.2, I.3, and I.4 illustrate other characteristics of the survey respondents. In addition to the information provided in the figures, 60% of the respondents had children, and 82% owned their own homes.

So, is our sample representative of everyone everywhere? Of course not. How about everyone in the United States? Again no. The participants are an excellent sample of what they are a sample of: mostly people working in larger organizations (both for-profits and nonprofits), with educational levels higher than the average of the general population, who are willing to spend their energy—and often their own time—pursuing free personal development that can help them in their careers.

Figure I.1. Level of Education Reported by Survey Respondents.

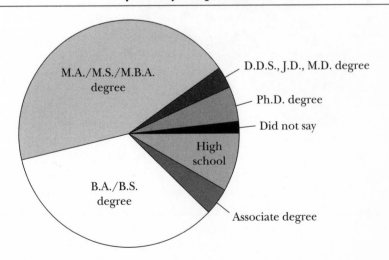

**Figure I.2. Management Responsibility
Reported by Survey Respondents.**

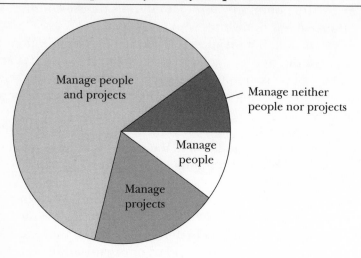

**Figure I.3. Time Spent in Management
Reported by Survey Respondents.**

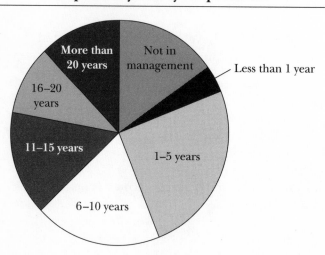

Figure I.4. Survey Respondents' Marital Status.

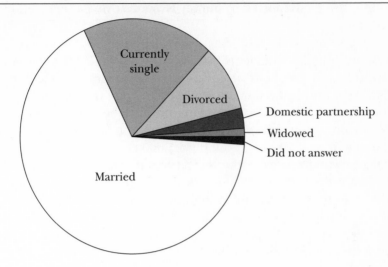

Why No Generalizations Are True, Including This One

All generalizations are dangerous, even this one.
—Alexandre Dumas, 1824–1895

Now that you know who participated in this study, it is important to explain that no matter how many people you survey or how good your statistics are, there are always going to be some people who don't fit the general description. In other words, *no principles are* always *true, including the ones you will read about in this book.*

The easiest way to think about this is in terms of distributions, and an example. The generalization: men are taller than women. Most people would agree that men are, on average, taller than women. Is every man taller than every woman? No. Is every man taller than most women? No. Are some women taller than most men? Yes. We can almost always think of some individual who does not fit the generalization, but that doesn't mean the generalization is nonsense. What it does mean is that any generalization that asserts it is correct every time for every person everywhere is definitely incorrect. (Except that all people breathe air . . . thus no generalizations are true, even the generalization that no generalizations are true!)

One of the issues with social science research is that we can almost never make statements that are hard-and-fast "rules" the way hard scientists can. Hard scientists have basic rules of science that work every time—and they know that on the rare occasions that the rules don't work, either something new has been discovered or the person running the experiment messed up. To take a standard example from chemistry, if you burn 1,000 grams of methane (natural gas), you'll get 2,743 grams of carbon dioxide and 2,246 grams of water every time you do it—unless the sample is contaminated. Our confidence isn't quite as high in social science because people are much less predictable than chemicals in a beaker, and we can't predict with a greater than 99% level of certainty what any individual is going to do or know or believe.

What that means from a practical perspective is that there are always people who are exceptions to the standard pattern; there are always a few men who are shorter than almost all women, and a few women who are taller than almost all men. So what happens is that as you do this type of research, you automatically add in "weasel words" almost every other sentence because you understand that what you are saying, though true on average, is not true for everybody everywhere. And you know that if you don't insert caveats constantly, someone is going to convert an unweaseled statement into a universal truth.

So in an attempt to avoid (1) readers' taking anything said in this book as absolutely true of every person in a particular category, and (2) having to put conditional statements around every comment we make in this book (which would be as tedious to read as it would be to write), let me say the following now, and please insert it (mentally) every time you see a generalization or principle:

> **This is true for many—perhaps most—people,
> under many—perhaps most—circumstances,
> but it isn't true for everyone, everywhere,
> in every circumstance.
> And just because we can all think of someone
> who doesn't fit perfectly with this explanation
> doesn't invalidate the principle.**

Before You Proceed . . .

This book presents ten principles. But in the course of our research, we also discovered an underlying theme that informs each and every principle we'll present. This theme doesn't spring from any individual piece of data we collected; rather, it becomes clear when you look at the pattern of results as a whole. It is the most parsimonious explanation for the generational conflict we hear people talk about and see at work. We alluded to it earlier; here we'll describe it so that you can identify it more clearly when reading through the principles:

> **Most intergenerational conflict shares
> a common point of origin: the issue of
> clout—who has it, who wants it.**

As we were doing our research, it became clear that fundamentally, generational conflict and comments about unacceptable behavior on the part of another generation often stem from a particular group's notion that it gets to make the rules and that the other group has to follow these rules. If the rules are being challenged, so too is the superior position and stature of the people who believe they get to make the rules that others then have to follow.

Our research revealed that in the U.S. workplace, older people generally think they should get to make the rules, and they think that the younger people should follow their rules. No surprises there. For example, people often complain about how some younger person wears casual clothes to work. The criticism is that the clothes are "inappropriate" or "unprofessional." In whose opinion? Obviously in the opinion of the people who are doing the criticizing. Have you ever noticed people seldom talk about how odd the workplace behavior of the older generation is in comparison with the younger generation? What would happen if masses of people in their 50s wore jeans and T-shirts to work? Would it suddenly become acceptable, or would the people in their 20s start complaining about the "unprofessional" attire? It is possible, but it isn't likely. Though younger people have opinions about other generations and make negative comments about older people, the behavior the older generation accepts is considered the standard. So younger people's comments (in the example above) about the older people's "unprofessional" attire would be seen as illegitimate griping and a grab for control rather than as legitimate complaints about inappropriate workplace behavior.

In another example, when does conflict between parent and child stop being attributed to typical disagreements that any people have when living in close quarters, and start being attributed to a generation gap? The gap appears when the children (typically teenagers) begin to see themselves as having opinions that are different from those of their parents but no less valid just because they are younger. In essence, the generation gap appears when the younger people stop accepting everything the older group tells them and starts believing that their own opinions, perspectives, and attitudes have validity equal to those of their elders. The result of this belief is that the generation gap exists only when the younger generation ceases to follow the rules set down by the older generation. As long as the younger generation complies, no gap exists.

But (theoretically) everyone in the workplace is an adult who is being paid to do a job and is therefore equal except for positional authority assigned by the organization (that is, his or her level in the organization). But, as in Orwell's *Animal Farm,* some people believe they are more equal than others, and they use what attributes they have (for example, age, political acumen, organizational tenure) to increase their clout within the organization. As organizations increasingly promote younger people over older people (thus increasing the positional power of the younger people), older people naturally work to maintain the balance of power—in their favor—by using their greater age and experience. One way they do this is to comment negatively about the bad behavior of younger people (thus making specific individuals look bad by association). Another way they do this is to use the behavior of their own generation as the model for appropriate behavior (thus making themselves look good by association).

People of the older generation also maintain their clout by emphasizing the value of their experience. Experience is perceived both by people and by organizations as valuable because it is believed to be synonymous with knowledge. But it isn't. Now, don't misunderstand us—we think experience is critically important. We also think that on average, people with more experience (older people) know more than do people with less experience (younger people). However, *what is important about experience is how one processes it and what knowledge one gains from it, not just having it.* Just having existed through experiences doesn't make someone more knowledgeable or more successful.

For example, organizations have been trying to figure out for decades what makes a person successful as an expatriate. One of the most interesting findings from all the research on expatriates is that past experience as an expatriate is not a good predictor of future success as an expatriate. Success actually depends on how well the individual processed the experience and how much he or she learned from it. So experience is important, but only in how much is learned from it—and that skill is not related to age.

Similarly, younger people criticize older ones for being resistant to new ideas or unwilling to embrace technology. "The number of gray cells goes down as the number of gray hairs goes up," some say. Others claim that older people are "out of touch" (and therefore less attuned to the client). Although the argument is about trying new things rather than about experience, what underlies the criticism is still the desire to increase clout.

Thus the generation gap enters the workplace, getting blamed for conflicts that really have nothing to do with fundamental generational differences (bad behavior exists in people of *all* ages) and everything to do with the natural desire of older people to maintain their clout and the desire of younger people to increase their clout.

So as you read the chapters that follow, and as you consider the conflicts that arise between people of different generations in the course of your work, take the time to consider the clout factor. Often the accusatory language you hear directed at one generation or another has its roots in broader issues of confidence and security. Often the complaints about "not being taken seriously" or about "behaving as if they're entitled" (whether directed at the young or the old) are actually masking fear of potential loss of clout, *not* reflecting significant fundamental differences among the generations.

All Generations Have Similar Values; They Just Express Them Differently

Many people talk about enormous differences in values between older and younger people as if these differences were an established fact. They say things like

- The younger generation has no values.
- The current lack of values among young people in the workplace is contributing to the general decline of organizations.
- The value system is different than it used to be.

In fact, when we were formulating our research plans, we heard people say such things so often—and with more conviction than evidence—that we set up a line of inquiry just about values.

The idea that generations have fundamentally different values is obviously a commonly held belief. But, we asked ourselves, is it true? Are there significant values differences among the generations? If there are, what are those differences? And if there aren't major differences, what is causing the "generational values gap" at work?

Research

To evaluate what values people said were most important to them, we set up a computer program that presented people with 40 values in such a way that they had to prioritize some values over others.

After this process, each individual ended up with a "top ten" list of values among the 40 values available. Using these lists, we identified the values that people said were most important to them. We were also able to isolate the values that were least important. And we were able to sort and compare these results by the age of the individuals participating.

In this part of our research, 1,285 people responded (68 Silents, 316 Early Boomers, 410 Late Boomers, 411 Early Xers, and 80 Late Xers).

Top Ten Values

The values chosen in the top ten most frequently were

FAMILY (72%)

INTEGRITY (65%)

ACHIEVEMENT (48%)

LOVE (48%)

COMPETENCE (47%)

HAPPINESS (46%)

SELF-RESPECT (45%)

WISDOM (45%)

BALANCE (39%)

RESPONSIBILITY (38%)

Of these values, only FAMILY and INTEGRITY were chosen by more than half of the people surveyed. It is interesting to note that there is not overall agreement on what the most important values are. There is no consensus among respondents that a certain set of values is more important than all the other values. Furthermore, there was no agreement even within any of the generations that one set of values was significantly more important than another. (Table 1.1 shows the top ten values as reported by the different generations.) The main message here is that *there is not strong agreement among individuals about which specific values are the most important.*

Table 1.1. Top Ten Values, by Generation.

Silents	Early Boomers	Late Boomers	Early Xers	Late Xers
INTEGRITY 69%	INTEGRITY 70%	FAMILY 76%	FAMILY 78%	FAMILY 78%
WISDOM 60%	FAMILY 60%	INTEGRITY 72%	INTEGRITY 60%	LOVE 73%
SELF-RESPECT 59%	WISDOM 57%	ACHIEVEMENT 53%	HAPPINESS 52%	HAPPINESS 59%
FAMILY 53%	SELF-RESPECT 48%	COMPETENCE 50%	ACHIEVEMENT 50%	SELF-RESPECT 58%
COMPETENCE 47%	COMPETENCE 48%	LOVE 47%	LOVE 49%	FRIENDSHIP 53%
RESPONSIBILITY 41%	ACHIEVEMENT 45%	WISDOM 45%	COMPETENCE 46%	HELP OTHERS 46%
LOVE 40%	LOVE 44%	HAPPINESS 45%	SELF-RESPECT 43%	RESPONSIBILITY 41%
JUSTICE 38%	HAPPINESS 40%	SELF-RESPECT 41%	BALANCE 43%	LOYALTY 41%
ACHIEVEMENT 35%	BALANCE 37%	BALANCE 41%	RESPONSIBILITY 37%	INTEGRITY 39%
CREATIVITY 34%	RESPONSIBILITY 36%	RESPONSIBILITY 39%	WISDOM 36%	WISDOM 34%

Do generations have different values?

No, they really don't. Some people from each generation chose each of the values.

When you look at all 40 values that people could choose, the most striking result is how similar the generations are in their values priorities (see Appendices A and B). Although there are a few differences, overall we can't say that the generations have different values.

For example, the value ACHIEVEMENT is not chosen much more frequently by Early Boomers than it is by Early Xers, so it isn't accurate to say that Early Boomers are more focused on achievement. However, it is chosen significantly more frequently by Late Boomers and Early Xers than it is by Silents. Similarly, BALANCE is not chosen much more often by Early Xers than it is by Early or Late Boomers, so it would be incorrect to say that Early Xers are more focused on balance than Early or Late Boomers are, but they do choose it more frequently than Late Xers do.

Overall, FAMILY was chosen more often than any other value. Even so, it was chosen in the top ten by only 72% of those who responded. What does that say about the other 28%? (Author's Note: We were shocked that 28% of people didn't put FAMILY in their top ten. We checked and rechecked the data, and the result is real. Our best guess is that some people really don't think family is important, and that others meant FAMILY when they included LOVE and HAPPINESS in their top ten.) FAMILY shows up more frequently for Late Boomers, Early Xers, and Late Xers than it does for Early Boomers and Silents. Does this mean that Early Boomers and Silents are less focused on their families, or is this pattern a result of a change in focus that comes with age (rather than generation)?

Overall, ACHIEVEMENT was chosen in the top ten by 48% of those who responded—slightly more often than HAPPINESS and WISDOM. ACHIEVEMENT was chosen more frequently by Early Boomers, Late Boomers, and Early Xers than it was by Silents and Late Xers. Does this mean that Silents and Late Xers are less interested in achievement, or that they are at a point in their careers and lives where that is less of a focus?

Overall, COMPETENCE, HAPPINESS, SELF-RESPECT, and WISDOM were chosen about equally frequently (45% to 46%).

FAME was chosen in the top ten by only 3% of those who responded. Early and Late Xers chose it more frequently than did the older generations. Perhaps this is a result of youthful dreams that have not yet gone away?

COMPETITION was also chosen in the top ten by only 3% of those who responded. Late Boomers and Early Xers chose it more frequently than other generations did. Perhaps this is a result of career stage because those two generations are more in the throes of jockeying for position in their careers than are any of the other generations.

AUTHORITY was chosen in the top ten by 6% of those who responded. Silents chose it more often than any other generation did.

What is clear from these results is that many of the standard stereotypes aren't supported by the data—that generational stereotypes are about as true as *any* stereotype is.

Top Three Values

Overall, the values that show up in respondents' top three most frequently are

FAMILY (60%)

LOVE (31%)

INTEGRITY (28%)

SPIRITUALITY (21%)

SELF-RESPECT (17%)

HAPPINESS (17%)

ACHIEVEMENT (13%)

BALANCE (11%)

ECONOMIC SECURITY (11%)

WISDOM (9%)

COMPETENCE (9%)

When you look at the values that each of the generations chose most frequently for the top three (as shown in Table 1.2 and Appendix B), what you find is that there are large similarities and a few interesting small differences.

Table 1.2. Top Three Values, by Generation.

Silents	Early Boomers	Late Boomers	Early Xers	Late Xers
FAMILY 46%	FAMILY 45%	FAMILY 64%	FAMILY 67%	FAMILY 73%
INTEGRITY 46%	INTEGRITY 32%	INTEGRITY 29%	LOVE 32%	LOVE 49%
LOVE 26%	LOVE 27%	LOVE 29%	INTEGRITY 24%	SPIRITUALITY 28%
SPIRITUALITY 25%	SPIRITUALITY 21%	SPIRITUALITY 23%	HAPPINESS 20%	HAPPINESS 25%
SELF-RESPECT 22%	SELF-RESPECT 21%	HAPPINESS 18%	SPIRITUALITY 17%	FRIENDSHIP 25%
JUSTICE 15%	ECONOMIC SECURITY 15%	ACHIEVEMENT 16%	SELF-RESPECT 16%	SELF-RESPECT 19%
WISDOM 15%	COMPETENCE 14%	SELF-RESPECT 14%	ACHIEVEMENT 14%	HELP OTHERS 13%
RESPONSIBILITY 10%	WISDOM 13%	BALANCE 11%	BALANCE 13%	INTEGRITY 11%
BALANCE 9%	HAPPINESS 13%	ECONOMIC SECURITY 10%	ECONOMIC SECURITY 9%	ECONOMIC SECURITY 8%
ECONOMIC SECURITY 9%	ACHIEVEMENT 12%	WISDOM 10%	FRIENDSHIP 8%	LOYALTY 6%

FAMILY was chosen in the top three by 60% of respondents. All generations chose it most frequently, but this was more prominent for younger generations than it was for older generations.

HAPPINESS was chosen in the top three by 17% of respondents overall, and was chosen much more frequently by the younger generations (Late Boomers, Early Xers, and Late Xers) than it was by the older generations (Silents and Early Boomers). Does this show a generational shift in the importance of the concept of happiness in people's lives, or is this an effect of age?

WISDOM was chosen in the top three by 9% of respondents overall, and was chosen more frequently by the older generations. Only 1% of Late Xers chose it as one of their top three values, while 15% of Silents chose it.

ECONOMIC SECURITY was chosen in the top three by 11% of respondents overall, and Early Boomers chose it much more frequently than did any other generation. Perhaps this is an indication of concerns about eventual retirement.

ACHIEVEMENT was chosen in the top three by 13% of those who responded; Early Boomers, Late Boomers, and Early Xers were more likely to put ACHIEVEMENT in their top three than were Silents and Late Xers.

What Happened to Spirituality?

Why is SPIRITUALITY on the list of most important values when it wasn't in the top ten list? Because people either think it is very important (rating it in their top three) or don't think it is critical (ranking it below the top ten). Overall, 29% of people put SPIRITUALITY in their top ten, and 21% put it in their top three. This means that 71% of people didn't rank SPIRITUALITY above 11, 8% ranked it 4–10, and 21% put it in their top three. In other words, most people either think spirituality is central to their values system (the 21%) or do not choose it as a value at all (the 71%).

The overall message is that there are at least as many similarities among the generations in their values choices as there are differences. What we hear day after day is that there is a gap the size of the Grand Canyon between the values of older and younger people. (Specifically, we hear that older people have values and younger people don't.) So when we found that older and younger people were expressing the same primary values in their responses, we had to start thinking about what it meant that the values weren't different. If both older and younger people say they value the same things, why do people think the values of different generations are so different? Because people from different generations behave differently, and people think that behavior equals values or values equal behavior.

Neither is true. Values are what you *believe* is important, not what you *do* to express those beliefs. People often think that if you have one set of values, you will behave one way; if you behave differently from that way, it obviously means you have a different set of values. But that isn't always true, and perceived generational differences are excellent examples of how people use different behaviors to express the same values. The generations don't differ in what they value; they differ in how they demonstrate those values.

> By nature, men are nearly all alike;
> By practice, they get to be wide apart.
> —CONFUCIUS (551–479 B.C.)

So let's summarize by answering a few fundamental questions:

- Do the different generations have different values?

  No, they really don't. There are a few differences, but the primary values people hold are the same.

- If there aren't fundamental differences between the values of Silents, Early Boomers, Late Boomers, Early Xers, and Late Xers, why do people think that there are differences?

  Because how people express their values is often different by generation, just as it is often different by culture. For example, wearing jeans to work may be considered to be an expression of disrespect for the work site to a Silent or an Early Boomer who thinks that jeans are too informal for work, but to employees from the Early or Late Xer generations, wearing jeans at work is not necessarily an expression of disrespect—they just want to wear jeans.

All Generations Have Similar Values; They Just Express Them Differently

What has become clear through the research and through talking to people is that conflicts about values are not about the values themselves but about how people express those values. So with regard to values issues, younger people are not contributing to the decline of the working world any more than older people are. Further, you don't have to be concerned about how to cater to each generation individually. The values of the generations are so similar that there is nothing you need to do to hedge against the "bad" values of one generation or to try to keep the "good" values of another. The values are the same. However, the behaviors that go along with those values are different.

> *Our sires' age was worse than our grandsires'.*
> *We their sons are more worthless than they:*
> *So in our turn we shall give the world a progeny yet more corrupt.*
> —HORACE (QUINTUS HORATIUS FLACCUS, 65–8 B.C.)

As a leader, you need to be aware of differences in behavior among the generations. As we've said, it isn't what people *say* they believe in that causes problems between members of different generations; it's what they *do* that causes the conflicts. Perceived values conflicts between people of different generations can arise in a number of different ways.

Fundamental Difference in Values

This is as likely to happen between people of the same generation as it is between people of different generations. For example, Boomers on average don't agree with each other about what values are important any more than they agree with the Xers or

Silents. Differences among individuals on what values are important are the rule rather than the exception.

> Tim and John are working together to produce a better advertising campaign for their company. Tim is consistently focused on making sure that everyone involved in the project is happy about what is going on. John is consistently focused on producing a campaign that is good and that will get attention for the company—therefore making the company money. As an internal, company-based deadline looms, these values come into conflict because the artwork is substandard. (Amy, who created the artwork, misunderstood what she was supposed to produce, and she delivered it at the last minute so there wasn't time to redo it.)
>
> John wants the deadline pushed back so that the artwork can be redone and the campaign will be successful—and if they have to explain that they must push back the deadline because Amy's work wasn't right, so be it. Tim insists that the deadline stay the same, and says that the artwork is good enough. Tim believes it is more important to meet the internal deadline and avoid having Amy get into trouble for misunderstanding the instructions than it is to have the campaign be very good.
>
> Tim and John are at an impasse because John thinks it is more important that the work be done well and the campaign be good (competence is the priority, not "good enough"), and Tim thinks it is more important that the deadlines be met and Amy's poor work not be brought up because it would upset her (affiliation is the priority).

Working with people who have fundamentally different values is tough. If Tim and John can recognize that they hold different values, they can work to resolve the conflict by

- Compromise
- One of the two leaving the project
- One of the two changing his values

Most likely the fundamental difference of opinion won't be resolved; it is unlikely that Tim will begin to prioritize competence over affiliation or that John will prioritize affiliation over competence. The most likely outcome is that they will come to a compromise that each will be equally happy (or unhappy) with.

Another possibility is that John will eventually stop working with Tim because he will become increasingly frustrated with having to compromise all the time. What is least likely is that one of the two will change his values.

What actually happened? Tim got what he wanted: the campaign was turned in before the deadline, and nothing happened to Amy. John decided that having a good campaign was important enough to him that he was willing to do extra work to achieve it, so he arranged the process so that the artwork could be completely redone in the next stage. There were additional costs to the project because John had to hire a new artist and do a lot of extra work, but in the end he felt it was worth the extra effort and was pleased with the product.

Same Value, Different Expressions

As we've noted, people who share the same value can express that value in different ways, which may lead to conflict. For example, varying expressions of the value of collaboration can lead to conflict.

> Kim and Jerry work in the same company in different divisions. In this company, collaboration is considered to be a very important value. Both Kim and Jerry agree that collaboration is important, and they both say they work hard to make sure they behave in a collaborative way. Nonetheless, they are often unhappy with each other because Jerry thinks that Kim doesn't actually collaborate.
>
> Jerry's perspective is that Kim doesn't value collaboration. He believes that she really wants to be able to make all the decisions herself. He thinks this is obvious, and as evidence he cites how she resists inviting people to meetings and avoids consulting people about the decisions she is making. He believes that she just wants to go with her gut instinct rather than ask for other people's opinions.
>
> Kim believes she is very collaborative. As evidence she points to her inviting people to meetings and asking for others' opinions all the time. She believes that the fact that she doesn't ask everyone in the building to every meeting or take a vote of all staff for every decision doesn't mean she's not being collaborative. She says that she is interested in other opinions and doesn't know what else Jerry wants her to do to be collaborative.

So, is one of these people collaborative and the other not? Is Jerry so touchy-feely he probably never gets anything done because he's asking everyone for opinions and having endless meetings? Is Kim too power hungry to collaborate with others? Or do they just have different ideas of what being collaborative means when it comes to what people actually do at work?

Some people would claim that the difference between these two people is fundamentally a values issue: one person values collaboration, the other doesn't. In this case, what is actually going on is that they are expressing the value differently. Kim and Jerry both value collaboration, but they have very different ideas about what it means to act collaboratively in the workplace.

Given what we now know about the true nature of the conflict, what might Kim and Jerry do to solve their problems?

They might begin by discussing what they each define as collaborative behavior. If they can understand what each thinks is collaborative, then they can better identify where they disagree. And if they know how their perspectives are divergent, they can do a better job of figuring out where they need to be compromising and thinking about what the other needs.

It would also be helpful if Jerry would hold his tongue when he finds himself about to say that Kim doesn't value collaboration. If Jerry feels strongly about including more people in meetings or making decisions differently, he would do better to explain to Kim exactly why he believes that his approach would be more productive than hers. For example, does he see real difficulty in getting initiatives through because Kim doesn't include enough people in the decision making? Or is his concern primarily about helping people feel more "heard" within the group? Jerry would be more persuasive if he could explain to Kim—without using generalizations or critical language—what the improved outcome would be from a change in her behavior.

Kim, for her part, might try to step back and figure out what is motivating Jerry's need to include more people in the meetings and decision making. Is there something specific that he thinks is going wrong because of her behavior? Can he show times when something would have gone more smoothly if more people were brought in to the decision-making process? Or is this a personal issue with him? Is it that Jerry feels as though he doesn't have enough of a say in the decisions, and is accusing Kim of not being collaborative as a backhanded way to get her to give him more power? If Kim can figure out Jerry's motives, she can address his concerns more effectively.

Whether or not you agree with another person's (opposing) perspective, that perspective is very useful information to have. Both Jerry and Kim can use the disagreement to better understand the other's viewpoint, values, and goals, and the other's ideas about how those goals might be most effectively accomplished. The feedback people give you is always useful, because it tells you something about how others see you or about others' motivations. In any case, you can use the information to help bridge the differences in perspectives in a way that is advantageous to both parties. What Kim, Jerry, and probably many of us need to work on is how we deliver the information and how we hear it ourselves.

How family is valued is another area that often results in conflict because people have different ways of expressing the same value. FAMILY was the value chosen most frequently, with 34% of the respondents choosing it as their first value (the most important value on the list to them), 60% putting it in their top three, and 72% putting it in their top ten. But when you ask people from different generations what valuing family translates into in their day-to-day behavior, their responses often sound as if they come from different planets. Older men (Silents and often both the Early and Late Boomers) are likely to say they show that they value their family by working long hours and making a lot of money so that their families can have what they want.

In contrast, Early and Late Xers are likely to say they show that they value their family by spending more time with their families (even though they don't actually work fewer hours). There is much less focus on the amount of money they're bringing home and much more focus on the time they get to enjoy with their families.

Sometimes this difference in how people express their valuing of family can result in different attributions about why people are working as much (or as little) as they are. One stereotypical conclusion is that those who work many hours and are working hard to climb the corporate ladder are selfish workaholics; in fact, their real motivation may be to provide a good and stable financial life for their families. Another stereotypical conclusion is that those who don't work many hours are lazy slackers; their real motivation may be to spend more time with their families. Remembering that people might be expressing the same values in different ways, in view of different contexts and different economic pressures, can serve as an antidote to making these kinds of stereotypical attributions.

How This Applies to You

The research shows that the generations' values do not differ significantly—individuals of all generations differ much more from each other than any generation does from the others. That is, there are more differences within each generation than there are between generations. Therefore, when you are party to a conflict that appears to be about generation-based values differences, you need to try to remember two things. First, it is more likely that the conflict is about a difference between individuals that has nothing whatsoever to do with their generation. Second, the conflict is about differences in behavior rather than about a fundamental values difference.

For example, at the beach today (in the United States) a woman considers herself to be dressing modestly if she wears a tank suit (one-piece) rather than a bikini. Sixty years ago, the smallest, most revealing bathing suits were more concealing than the most modest ones are today. We need to remember that it is better to assume that the values are the same and work from there.

A pertinent example has shown up recently in the courts. More and more people (especially younger people) are getting facial piercings and showing visible tattoos at work. What does it mean to have a tattoo or facial piercing? What are the values expressed by that choice? We're sure that if you think about this topic, you'll have some gut-level reaction to it. And the question is becoming more relevant every day as tattoos and piercings become more prevalent in different areas of society and as they are being seen more by clients.

The issue has come up many times in the courts, typically around the question of how much the organization can control the appearance of individual workers to protect the image of the organization. There was a recent court decision in which a woman sued, alleging sex discrimination. The core of the case was that she had a tattoo and was required to cover it, but a male coworker was not required to cover his. Why the different treatment? The company felt that other people thought that men with tattoos (especially military ones) were heroes, whereas women with tattoos were "bad" (that is, prostitutes or drug users). The court decided that the company's behavior was based on outdated gender stereotypes that were inadequate justification for treating men and women differently.

What the company was doing was what people do every day when they see another's behavior and attribute a particular set of values to it. The fundamental flaw in this thinking is that we can't possibly determine another person's values simply from observation of his or her behavior, or clothing, or piercings. We can know what it would mean if *we* behaved that way, but we can't possibly know—without asking—what it means for the other person to behave that way.

If You Are a Manager

If you are a manager faced with employees who are at odds over a seeming values conflict, ask yourself first whether it really is a values issue. Is the conflict about fundamental differences in values, or is it about feeling valued and respected? Is it about what behaviors show respect? Is it about certain employees not being treated the way they think they should be treated? Is it about them thinking that they should have power (and seniority) over someone who they feel should not have it? Often what at first glance appear to be values conflicts are really more about people feeling valued and respected by the people they work with. As a manager, you have to decide how much of the conflict is fixable and how much people are just going to have to tolerate. If you can intervene (quietly, often with each party individually) and coach the parties to help them understand what is going on with the other person, you have both helped yourself in potentially reducing workplace conflict and provided a learning opportunity for the people involved. Every opportunity to take the perspective of others is a learning opportunity, for there are few skills more useful to people than being able to accurately "read" and react to others around them. The earlier a person learns this, the more effective they will be. The better they are at this skill, the fewer of this type of conflict they are likely to have.

Sometimes the issue isn't going to be fixable, because someone believes the other is just wrong and can't see the situation from any other perspective. As a manager in these cases, you might find it useful to understand why employees who make values judgments think that they have the right (read: status) to do so. Employees have a right to personal opinions about the people they work with, but these opinions cannot be allowed to affect the productivity of the group. Most of the time, people can manage these perceived values differences just fine—after all, they don't have to like everyone they work with. When they can't, you as the manager need to diagnose the true origin of the conflict (because it generally isn't actually about values) and help people deal with the real root of the problem.

It is true that people from different generations often express their values differently and that these different expressions of values can cause conflict. When these problems surface, you can remind those involved that differences in behavior do not necessarily reflect differences in fundamental values. As a leader, you need to help everyone remember that there is a difference between values and behaviors. If the people are actually complaining about behaviors, find out what is bothering them. Help them move away from general complaints about "values" and understand the specific behaviors that are troubling them. If you can help them understand the particular issue, you can help all the parties involved put together an action plan or a behavior plan so that the conflicts don't arise—or, if they do, can be dealt with more effectively and efficiently.

When you hear someone saying that younger people "have no values," ask her whether she really thinks that or whether she just doesn't like what a particular younger person is doing at that moment. Do the people saying this really think that it is the younger person's fundamental values that are wrong, or is it just how they are behaving at the time? If the complaint centers on how the younger person is behaving, ask the person making the comment (in a lighthearted way) why he thinks that he is the arbiter of "good" values in the workplace. It is one thing to make such complaints at church or at home, but a workplace is different. Everyone is of course entitled to an opinion but needs to be circumspect about expressing personal condemnations at work. Addressing work issues is fine, but it is not a good idea to make sweeping stereotyping statements about coworkers.

It is important for us always to remember that even when people (older or younger) are doing things that drive us crazy or offend our sense of what is right, it is likely that they are doing what they are doing out of values very similar to ours . . . they're just expressing them in an exceptionally annoying way! We can't say they are without values and are therefore bad people—it is no more true of them than it is of us.

What You Should Have Learned from This Chapter

- People of all generations have similar values.
- FAMILY is the value chosen most frequently.
- Values and behaviors aren't the same thing—someone can behave very differently from you and still hold the same values.

Everyone Wants Respect; They Just Don't Define It the Same Way

We're sure everyone has heard someone complain that there is too little respect shown in organizations. The typical complaint is that younger people are disrespectful of the people they should be showing respect for—mainly older employees and people in authority. Others complain that older people are just as bad, that older people have respect only for older people or for people higher in the hierarchy. The complaint is that older people appear to think that people deserve different amounts of respect, primarily depending on how much gray hair they have or how much money they make.

A few years ago, I was in Australia talking about how the different generations had roughly the same values. After the presentation a man came up to me and said that I was wrong because he had a specific example that demonstrated how different the generations' values were.

The man said, "At my company there is a young man who obviously doesn't respect others. You can tell this because he is no more polite to the president of his company than he is to the receptionist at the front desk. How can you say that there is no difference between the generations when this young man shows no more respect to the president of the company than he does to the receptionist?"

So I asked him, "Is the young man rude to either the receptionist or the president?"

"No," the man said, "he isn't impolite to either. He just treats the president of the company with the exact same amount of respect that he does the receptionist."

"What I'm hearing," I said, "is that he is just as polite to the receptionist as he is to the president of the company. How can you say he is being disrespectful, when he is respectful to both? Are you saying that if he were less respectful to the receptionist than he is to the president, that would be a better indication that he was a respectful person?"

Through this conversation (which went on for some time), it became clear that the older man took the equal amounts of respect being shown to people at all levels in the organization as an indicator of disrespect to the people higher in the organization. Therefore, he thought the younger man had "no respect" (his words) for the president of the organization.

A similar theme—and similar language—shows up in the musical *My Fair Lady,* when Eliza Doolittle accuses Henry Higgins of treating her like a scullery maid rather than like a lady, to which he replies that he treats a lady no better than he does a scullery maid, so what does she have to complain about? From his perspective, the only problem would be if he treated one better than another; if he treats them equally badly, then it shouldn't be an issue!

So what does "showing respect" really mean? Does it mean that you are more polite or subservient to someone who is more powerful than you are to someone who is much less powerful? Is being obsequious required to show respect? Is being curt to someone in a lower position required to show respect to people higher? When we looked at what people were saying and writing about respect, what we found was both revealing and frustrating.

There is, it turns out, a huge amount of discussion and discourse on the topic, most of which seems to conclude that the basic structure of organizational life is about to fall apart because a generation (or two) of younger employees is not appropriately respectful. There is *not,* however, much in the way of current literature that attempts to define respect or clarify what it means in practice, in the context of work.

We found this gap between chatter at Starbucks and research results to be an irresistible one. So, we decided to try to find out

- How upset people are, really, about lack of respect in the workplace.
- Whether people from older generations actually talk about the respect issue more than do people from younger generations.
- Whether people from the different generations mean the same thing when they talk about a lack of respect. (And what does "respect" look like, anyway?)

Research

We didn't ask survey respondents any specific questions about respect. What we did ask about was what conflicts they had with people from other generations, what challenges they were facing in their careers, and what their organizations needed to do to retain them. We received a number of revealing comments about respect in response to the three questions.

Respect and Generational Conflict

The comments about respect made by respondents from all generations centered on the ideas that (1) there was something wrong with the other group because of the way they behaved or (2) the other group (whether older or younger) was not treating "me" well. They focused on how there was obviously something wrong with the other group (typically younger people) because they didn't behave respectfully toward the people who were older or in positions of authority. There were also some comments from younger people about older people having little respect for younger people because they treated the younger people so poorly.

One substantial difference between the comments made by younger people and those made by older people about generational conflict with regard to respect was in what respondents appeared to mean when they wrote about respect. What people meant by respect fell into three categories: (1) listen to me; pay attention to what I have to say; (2) give my opinions the weight I believe they deserve; and (3) do what I tell you to do.

Older people primarily talked about respect in terms of *give my opinions the weight I believe they deserve* and *do what I tell you to do.* Younger respondents characterized respect more as *listen to me* and *pay attention to what I have to say.*

Respect as a Career Challenge

People of all generations talked about lack of respect as a challenge they face in their careers. Some comments focused on the difficulty older people have interacting with younger people who don't have much respect for management. The comments were not solely from older people in management; they were also from the younger people's colleagues. These older colleagues said they found it challenging to work with the younger people who were less respectful of management than the older people would prefer (or thought was appropriate).

> Younger employees have less respect for management,
> and that is hard for me to adjust to.
> —Early Boomer

Younger employees also commented about the lack of respect they felt in the workplace. They said they had some difficulty getting older workers to take them seriously. Some said that the people they worked either with or for appeared to have little respect for their abilities or performance, which these older workers demonstrated by not listening to them. Young managers commented on the difficulty they had getting older employees to respect them. According to them, performance wasn't enough to gain the respect of the older people.

> I have experienced some "age discrimination." Had things said to
> me like, "You can't possibly know what you are talking about. . . .
> You are just starting out. . . . You don't have enough experience."
> —Early Xer

> [I'm a] younger manager with least seniority working to gain
> the respect of my older, more experienced direct reports.
> —Early Xer

Finally, both younger and older people said they felt as if management didn't respect them and often felt as if they were being treated disrespectfully.

Lack of respect from superiors.
—Early Boomer

Leader has no respect for subordinates.
—Late Xer

Respect and Retention

There were as many comments about respect related to retention (for more on this topic, see Principle 8). Not surprisingly, people said they would be more likely to stay with their organization if the organization would

- Respect older people with experience (more than young people)
- Respect young people (respect their talent, if nothing else)

The data indicate that there is a fundamental conflict here, because many of the comments suggested that organizations should show more respect to older people than to younger people. Some respondents said that longevity and experience were more deserving of respect than other attributes. By contrast, some younger people suggested that organizations should show more respect for talent and initiative (which they said was more characteristic of younger people) than for longevity (which obviously is characteristic of older people). In essence, older respondents thought that experience should count for more than raw talent, and younger people thought that experience shouldn't count for more than raw talent.

Review

So, to answer the questions we asked earlier in the chapter:

Are people really upset about lack of respect in the workplace?
The intensity of the comments we received indicates that some people are very upset about the lack of respect they see and feel at work, though it wasn't a frequent comment. What was notable was

that lack of respect showed up as a complaint in response to questions about generational conflict, career challenges, *and* retention, which suggests that it is relevant beyond the issue of generational conflict. We'll talk more about this topic in the chapter on retention (Principle 8).

***Do people from older generations talk about the respect
issue more than do people from younger generations?***

Yes, Silents and Early Boomers bring up respect as an issue about a third more often than do Late Boomers, Early Xers, and Late Xers. However, the intensity of the comments (if not the frequency) indicates that the younger generations also feel strongly about this subject.

***Do people from different generations mean the same
thing when they talk about a lack of respect?***

No, they don't. When Silents and Early Boomers (and some of the Late Boomers) talk about respect, what they are asking for is deference and special treatment. When Early and Late Xers (and some of the Late Boomers) talk about respect, what they are asking for is either esteem or to be listened to—they have no expectation that anyone should defer to them.

Everyone Wants Respect, They Just Don't Define It the Same Way

People (of every generation) have in their minds some idea of how people should treat them—of what "showing respect" looks like. When another's behavior does not conform to this expectation, people feel disrespected. The other's intention is irrelevant; that is, a person need not *deliberately* behave rudely to be perceived as disrespectful. It is his or her failure to meet expectations that is upsetting.

> One team member does not respect or value "young" co-workers;
> however, I am not certain if this person respects anyone.
> —Early Xer

> I am young, and the old people feel that you should
> treat them differently just because they are old.
> —Late Xer

Bad manners, meaning, not returning phone calls, e-mails, little
respect for how things should go in an orderly fashion.
—Late Boomer on how younger employees behave

So what do people mean when they say someone isn't showing
the proper respect in the workplace? What does it mean to show
respect for someone?

Older People Want Respect

When older people say they want respect, what they appear to
mean is that they want younger people to hold them in higher esteem (than they do others) and to defer to their perspectives.
Older survey respondents were not talking about just being listened to—they want the younger people to give more weight to
their opinions than younger people do to their own. Some also
consider questioning to be disrespectful.

My supervisor is of another generation. In my opinion, she has not
kept up with current regulations that are necessary to make some of
the decisions she is making. When I show her the new regulations, and
recommend ways of following them, conflict is created between us.
She feels that I am not experienced enough to be questioning her.
—Early Xer

[I am tired of] being ignored and having my opinions brushed
aside by my elders. How do you fight that without seeming
disrespectful? Being treated like a child. I realize I'm younger and
should show respect, but I was not born yesterday either.
—Early Xer

People in Authority Want Respect

The comments we received indicate that when people in positions
of authority say they want more respect than they are currently getting, many of them mean they want people to defer to them and
to obey them. It appears that some would prefer that employees—all
employees, not just younger or older ones—would stop doing things
that they perceive as questioning their authority. That includes

suggesting alterations to plans, suggesting other ways to do things, pointing out things they had missed, and suggesting that a decision wasn't the best one and needs to be rethought. Many people in authority think that work would get done much faster if employees would just do as they say and not ask so many questions. Many also think that decisions would get made more quickly if employees would just accept their position as the correct one and work from there immediately, rather than having to discuss all of the possible options.

> I feel that older workers tend to respond to my questions with mixed messages (i.e., they say one thing and act in another way). I feel that I am often perceived as a "troublemaker" even though each company I have worked within touts the value of "collaboration," "innovation," and "team building." I have found that disagreeing with the status quo often earns me this troublemaker moniker.
> —Early Xer

The reality is that management and leadership today require more than just a command-and-control approach. People don't work that way anymore—at least not in a lot of places. Many employees think about their work and what the implications of a particular decision are, rather than just doing what they are told, exactly how they are told to do it. When they believe that what they are being told to do isn't going to have the desired result, or when they see something they think could be done better, they're willing to point it out rather than just keeping quiet and assuming that whoever is in charge always knows best. Pointing out other ways to do things isn't about showing up management (at least not most of the time!); it is about making an honest, well-meant suggestion. And if you're thinking that some sectors don't have this problem, think again—it happens just about everywhere (though not necessarily with the same frequency).

The truth is that when people ask questions or provide suggestions, they are not deliberately setting out to be disrespectful. For most, showing disrespect is the last thing on their minds.

Younger People Want Respect

> People assume that because I am younger than they are that I could not possibly know/understand what the goal/outcome of a situation should be.
> —Early Xer

> I am tired of feeling as if you need to be here
> 25 years before your opinion counts.
> —Early Xer

The comments we received indicate that when younger people say they want respect, generally what they mean is that they want to be held in esteem and to have their opinions considered. They'd like other people to listen to them and to take their suggestions seriously. They think it is ridiculous that they have to be old before anyone will listen to their perspectives—especially when they think they have so many good ones to share! Like everyone else, they'd like people to defer to their opinions and to obey them, but they don't think it is likely to happen—in part because they don't do it themselves.

Younger people desperately want to do a good job and to contribute. They've been told that the way you do that is to participate and to be seen to participate, not just to keep your head down and do good work. In fact, standard advice to young people who want to move up in organizations is that the more you speak up (appropriately), the more likely you are to get ahead in organizations; just doing good work isn't enough anymore (if it ever was).

Furthermore, younger people have been taught that this is what they should be doing. Early education in the past twenty years has emphasized participation; children who offer solutions and suggestions and who are seen to actively participate receive more praise than those who sit back and wait for instruction and do solely what they are told. Younger people have been told for years that it is good for them to make suggestions—that any idea (even a bad one) is better than no idea at all. So when they make suggestions, they are trying to be helpful and to be seen as being helpful, not implying that someone is doing a lousy job or that they could do a better one. (Of course, there are some jerks who are trying to do just that, but they are in the minority.)

> Young men are fitter to invent than to judge,
> fitter for execution than for counsel, and fitter
> for new projects than for settled business.
> —FRANCIS BACON (1561–1626), *Essays*, 1925

> It seems that I'm treated differently because
> management sees me as the same age as their kids,
> and in turn talk down to me or at that level.
> —Late Xer

Some Boomers treat those younger than them as
children no matter the person's position or experience.
—Early Xer

When Authority Is Reversed

Workplace relationships become more complicated when someone younger manages someone who is older. Because people are
being promoted more frequently now on the basis of performance
rather than primarily because of seniority, there are more and
more instances of older employees reporting to younger ones. This
situation makes everyone uncomfortable because older people typically have higher status than younger people. Almost everyone is
brought up to defer to older people and to treat them with extra
respect. So what happens when older people report to younger
people? Some of the time it works, and some of the time it doesn't.
But nearly all the time both parties feel mildly uncomfortable because of the upside-down nature of their roles. It just feels as if
there is something vaguely wrong about a 55-year-old reporting to
a 25-year-old—even if the younger person really knows what she is
doing and does a stellar job. Consider the following example:

> Sue was given the "developmental assignment" of managing a matrix-based
> project team of 12; all but one of the members had 20 years more experience
> (and age) than she did. All of them came from her department, but they had
> reporting relationships to other people, so she had no positional authority
> at all.
>
> The project seemed to begin well. But as the work progressed, it became
> clear that the "team" really wasn't working as it should. The problem: one of
> the team members, Kathy, consistently didn't meet her deadlines—despite
> reminders and conversations both from Sue and from other members of the
> team.
>
> When the issue became acute—that is, when Kathy's tardiness threat-
> ened to derail the whole project—Sue called yet another meeting with Kathy
> to discuss the issue and to get an idea of what the problem was and what they
> could do to make sure the project was kept on track and the deadline was met.
>
> The meeting did not go well. Kathy (who was much older than Sue) got
> very angry (some would say she threw a tantrum) and told Sue that Sue had

no right to manage her—that Sue was younger than Kathy and that it was disrespectful of Sue to say anything negative at all. Kathy said that it didn't matter if she didn't meet the deadline. She said it was more important that Sue understand her position, which was lower than Kathy's (according to Kathy). Kathy said it didn't matter that Sue was the manager—because Sue was younger than Kathy, she'd just have to keep her opinions to herself and let Kathy do what she wanted. Further, Kathy said, Sue should understand how terribly disrespectful she was of Kathy, and she should know better than to criticize her elders.

Clearly there are several (at least) different management issues going on in this scenario. One is Kathy's anger about Sue's position of authority, given her age. Having the benefit of our research at our own fingertips, we might have anticipated that there would be conflicts because of different perceptions of respect. Unfortunately, these two didn't have the input of a research team and volumes of data on which to build a solution. So here's how the conflict actually played out:

After that explosive conversation with Kathy, Sue went to talk with her boss, Magda. Sue explained to Magda that Kathy had used Sue's age as a tool to attack Sue. Kathy was better able to use Sue's age because Sue had been given no positional authority over Kathy. Further, Sue reported, Kathy was insulted because someone younger (Sue) had been given responsibility for a project instead of her (Kathy). Sue said it didn't seem to matter to Kathy that she was going to be late; it was more important that Sue understand how disrespectful Sue was being by even discussing the issue.

Luckily Magda had been observing the team dynamics and knew what had happened. She told Sue that it wasn't Sue's fault, that Kathy had a reputation for not making her deadlines, and that she (Magda) wasn't surprised that Kathy had been so angry about being confronted with her lack of follow-through. Magda said that she had had similar experiences with Kathy, but that the organization had implicitly made a decision that Kathy was going to be allowed to continue to perform inadequately. There had been plenty of documentation about Kathy's nonperformance, and she was just passed from one department to the next. Magda told Sue that for Sue's team to make the deadlines, it was likely that Sue was going to have to do Kathy's work for her. Magda said that Sue could register a complaint with Kathy's boss before the next evaluation period, but that it was unlikely to have any effect on the situation.

Not a textbook management solution, by any means. But remember, this was real life. And the reality was that the problem was going to continue. Kathy wasn't going to be taken off the project and was not going to be held accountable for failing to do her work. Sue was going to be held accountable for Kathy's performance, as well as for any complaints Kathy had about Sue's management of the group. Magda made Sue feel understood and appreciated, but didn't actually do anything to end the problem. Nor did she help Sue find tools to fix the problem.

What's more, Kathy, Sue, and Magda might very well find themselves in the same situation next week. But what if they went forward armed with the results of our research? Suppose they were infused somehow with some clarity about what respect means to different generations and why Kathy might be feeling so threatened. (Suppose they had also read this book's discussion of this principle and had a sense of the power struggles and feelings of vulnerability underlying their interactions?) What might they do, going forward, to make things better (or at least tolerable) at work?

We'll start with Sue. Sue is perfectly justified in being annoyed that Kathy isn't doing her job. She is also perfectly justified in bringing to Kathy's attention the fact that the work hasn't been done. She does not deserve to be attacked by Kathy simply because Kathy feels cornered and doesn't like Sue's pointing out that Kathy hasn't done her work. Sue is perfectly justified in feeling offended by Kathy's behavior, and has done nothing wrong in trying to manage the project effectively.

But none of this actually helps Sue fix the problem. It would be helpful if Sue could understand why Kathy is so upset, because sometimes understanding the emotions or intentions behind a person's annoying behavior can help us not react as negatively to it. Sue can understand that Kathy is probably feeling cornered and annoyed at having been told she isn't doing her job. Kathy obviously believes (or says she believes) that age is more important than hierarchy within the organization. Basically Kathy is saying she doesn't care what the command structure is: her greater age trumps Sue's positional authority. If Sue can understand that perspective, she can begin to decide how to manage Kathy more effectively.

If Sue takes it as a given that Kathy resents Sue's position, Sue then needs to think about what leverage points she has. She cannot use her authority to make sure that Kathy does her job, but can Sue use social pressure to achieve her ends? Given that the other members of the team are getting their work done, perhaps a public meeting where all members explain what they have—and have not—done will force Kathy's hand. At such a meeting Kathy would have to explain to her age-peers on the team (not just to Sue) why Kathy has chosen not to do the work. Although Kathy has no respect for Sue's position or authority on the team because Sue is younger than Kathy, perhaps wanting respect from her age-peers will do enough to shame Kathy into getting the work done.

If Kathy continues not to get her work done, Sue can always go to Kathy and act as if she needs Kathy's help and coaching on how to meet the team's deadlines. Though some people would say it was manipulative, Sue's deliberately putting Kathy in a one-up position (vis-à-vis Sue) might be enough to smooth Kathy's ruffled feathers and get the work done. Sometimes for a younger manager, explicitly telling the older (unhappy) direct reports that the project needs *their* assistance, that *they* are a critical component, and that the work can't get done without *their* contribution because *they* know *so much* can go a long way toward solving the problem. Sometimes people just want to be appreciated, and a specific appeal to them that shows them how important they are to the process can take care of the problem.

Although you might think this approach is manipulative, it isn't in fact a lie—the work really *can't* get done without them, and you really do need and appreciate what they contribute. You may not think you should have to say it that way, but sometimes you do. If Sue can grasp that, she may be more effective working with Kathy (or people like her) in the future.

What about Kathy? It would be nice if Kathy believed she has an obligation to get work done when she says she'll get work done, especially when other people are relying on her. But in this organization she's been allowed to get away with not doing that, so why would she change her behavior now? It would also be nice if Kathy could think about the bad position she is putting Sue in. Sue has been put in charge and is going to be held responsible for what the group produces.

Whether or not Kathy thinks it is appropriate for Sue to be in her position, Kathy should ask herself whether she is actually *trying* to sabotage Sue's work just because she resents the fact that Sue was put in charge of the project. To that question, some people would say yes—that they are being that petty and that they think it is OK to "teach Sue a lesson" about "how things should be around here."

But many of the Kathys in this world would be horrified by the thought: they weren't *trying* to sabotage Sue; they just had other priorities—doing work for other (higher-ranking) people and projects—and thought the work for Sue's project was of less importance.

Finally, it would be useful if Kathy thought about the difference between home life and work life. There is no question that in most people's personal lives, older people have higher social status (greater gravitas) than younger people do. But work isn't home. At work, people are rewarded for different things than they are at home. People may not like it, but it is true. They may want to change the situation, but such change is unlikely. Fundamentally, organizations have moved to rewarding performance as well as tenure, and sometimes performance over tenure. Kathy needs to ask herself whether her response was reasonable *in the workplace.* Was her behavior professional? If she felt so strongly about this issue, why didn't she speak with her boss, rather than attacking someone whom she saw as being of lower status than she is?

We suggest that the real reason Kathy attacked Sue is that she knew she was in the wrong. It goes back to the clout issue discussed at the beginning of this book; Kathy attacked Sue about Sue's age because Kathy wanted something to even the power distribution and couldn't find it in organizationally sanctioned areas, such as performance or authority. So Kathy used what she had—the status she believes she should be afforded by being older—and attacked Sue. The question Kathy needs to ask herself is whether that behavior was really reasonable.

Finally, let's tackle Magda. Although Magda was sympathetic, she wasn't particularly helpful to Sue. What Magda did was to pacify Sue in the short term, but they could find themselves in the same position the next day or week. It would be better for Magda to force the organization to deal with the real (and apparently chronic) problem of Kathy's nonperformance. As long as Kathy is allowed to get away with not doing her job, she is likely to continue doing so.

At this point you probably want to know what happened. In the end, the work got done. Kathy did about 20% of what she was supposed to do, and Sue finished up the work, working many late nights and weekends to make sure that the final product was of the quality required by the organization. Magda was proud of the work Sue had done, and praised her work publicly to the organization. Sue was not given a raise or a bonus for the work. She was not promoted. Because she had done such a good job of making the work look seamless and had delivered on time, the organization didn't appreciate what she had had to do to get the job done. Sue is still with the organization. Magda eventually left. Kathy is still there, working for yet another division; she has, at this writing, the same reputation she had before. The organization continues to allow her to be passed around from division to division rather than address her performance problems. Sue feels lucky that she doesn't have to work with Kathy anymore, and has had no such problems since, with any other employees or colleagues.

How This Applies to You

The research shows that all of us—regardless of generation—want respect and believe that we deserve it. We want to know that the people we work with respect us, and we want to be treated with respect. Problems arise because we don't all define respect the same way. Understanding what people mean when they say they want respect and figuring out either how to get them the respect they want or how to modify their expectations so that they don't feel disrespected and resentful are challenges for anyone.

At Home and at Work

It is important to remember that the culture in the United States has taught us that older people should be deferred to, and that older people get to make the rules and younger people get to obey them. When you're at work, this is likely to be an issue when you're working in intergenerational groups.

Although at home older people might get to use the precedence that goes with age, at work they can't expect others to agree with them or to do what they say just because they are older. The quality of the message should be considered as much as the identity of the messenger. Experience doesn't make a bad argument good, and lack of experience doesn't make a good argument bad—the position should be evaluated on its own merits.

Questions Do Not Equal Disrespect

As we've noted, people's reaction to being questioned is another issue that often comes up. Some people think that an employee—of any generation—asking a question is (1) causing trouble, (2) being disrespectful, (3) trying to make the person in authority look bad, or a combination of these. Although it is true that sometimes people *do* ask questions for these reasons, the questions themselves can be helpful—regardless of whether or not they are asked for constructive reasons. There is an almost endless amount of research demonstrating that better decisions (of all types) are made when people feel free to ask questions.

What you need to figure out (and help others figure out) is whether there is anything useful in the question being asked—either in terms of producing something or your gaining understanding of the questioner's perspective. Here are some questions to consider when you find yourself getting annoyed by someone questioning you:

• *Is the person asking a question because she doesn't know the answer?* If someone honestly doesn't know the answer, it would be helpful to give it to her. Doing so would also improve your relationship with the person asking the question. If you don't know the answer, say so. In most cases you don't lose clout by not knowing the answer; you do lose clout by pretending to know the answer when you don't and being caught later.

• *Is the person asking a question because he is afraid of doing something wrong?* If he is, should he be? Is that how you want this person to feel? Sometimes such a feeling is appropriate, but other times people aren't as productive if they're always afraid you're going to get angry with them for doing something wrong.

• *Is the person asking a question because she doesn't feel that she was heard (or listened to) during a discussion?* Does this happen often with this person? Is this because the person is a time-hog, or because she really is being marginalized by the group? Is this person being ignored or pushed aside because she's perceived as being less "experienced"? Is she being ignored because she's perceived as being an old "fuddy-duddy"? Should she be listened to? If yes, what are you going to do to help support her to make sure she is heard? What is the point of having her on the team if her perspective isn't included? If she isn't a productive member of the team, why is she still there?

- *Is the person asking a question because he thought of something that he thinks might be helpful?* If so, respond accordingly. The intention is good, and the intention should be reinforced, regardless of whether or not the question was a good one. If the question could have been more helpful couched in a different way or asked at a different time, coach the person about how to do better next time, while reinforcing that you appreciated the intention this time. Also be sure to reinforce to others that asking questions is a good thing because it brings up issues that others may not have thought of. It is better to deal with the question now, rather than later as things are exploding in your face!

- *Is the person asking a question because she just likes to make trouble?* If she is, have you called her on it? Why do you think she's doing it? Does she feel marginalized by the group? Does she think that you shouldn't be in the position you are in? Is it actually a power play on her part to make you look bad? If you think it is, do you really think that the person is both smart and malicious enough to think of such a thing? If she just likes to make trouble, how is this helping get the work done? If the person's behavior isn't helping get the work done, why is she still on your team? What do you need to do about her?

What Sue Might Do Differently

Think back to the Sue-Kathy-Magda incident discussed earlier. With a better understanding of the generational and respect issues involved, what could Sue do differently next time? Sue could have approached Magda for background information about all team members before the project started, and would thus have had some idea that Kathy was not completely trustworthy when it came to getting the work done. Then, rather than presuming that everyone on the team would do their part of the work, Sue could have anticipated Kathy's being a problem. Armed with this information, Sue could have constructed the tasks and team process in such a way that Kathy (1) wouldn't have as central a piece of work and (2) would be publicly responsible to the team as a whole, rather than to Sue. Making Kathy publicly responsible to the team (and therefore her age-peers) rather than just to Sue could have helped avoid the age conflict Sue encountered.

With a better understanding of her own perspective about generational and respect issues, Kathy too could have improved the situation. If unwilling to report to someone younger than she was, she could have asked to be taken off the team. Initially she could have asked to be put in charge of the team, instead of Sue.

It is entirely possible, however, that the age and respect issues were just an excuse for Kathy to avoid work (apparently her habit already). It is also possible that Kathy actually wanted Sue to fail to show the organization that it was a bad idea to put someone so junior in charge of such an important project.

When the Mountain Won't Move

Although someone might understand on an intellectual level what we've been saying in this chapter, he might not be able to shake his gut feelings about what respect and disrespect look like. That is often what these points of conflict come down to. Even if you haven't already, it is quite likely that you will come across someone with this mind-set, who thinks you're being disrespectful no matter how many times you have told him what your intention is. There isn't much you can do about people who can't hear you or who have a bad reaction that cannot be shaken by all the logic in the world. All you can do in these situations is think about your own behavior and decide: (1) what you want out of the interaction with the person and (2) what you are willing to do to get what you want.

Are you willing to be what you consider to be "extra respectful" if it will achieve your ends? You need to understand what you are willing to do, what you won't do, and (therefore) what your real priorities are. Once you understand your priorities, dealing with people with this mind-set will be much easier because you will be able to be strategic in your everyday interactions with them in order to achieve your long-term goals.

If You Are a Manager

If you are a manager, you probably have to deal with people who you think are insufficiently respectful. Maybe it is a younger person whose cavalier attitude or constant questions just tick you off for no reason you can put your finger on. Or maybe it is an older person who seems to talk incessantly because he thinks he has so much to "teach" you—when you can't remember requesting the "lesson." People do things like this all the time, and as a manager you are expected to behave more professionally (read: graciously) than the people below you. On top of having to deal with these annoyances yourself, other people come to you expecting you to fix the problem (for example, stop the person from behaving that way). Sometimes you see the problem (because you are annoyed as well), and sometimes you don't.

Either way, your responsibility is to coach the people complaining (and the people they're complaining about) to help them gain greater insight into the situation. People often get so tied up in the implied insult or disrespect that they can't work their way through the problem. You are in a unique position because you are not a peer of the people involved. Because you are their manager, you can force them to think through the whole situation. Make sure to have the respect issue (the conflict) described in detail, and then coach the person on how to diagnose the underlying issue. What is it about respect (or the perceived lack thereof) that is causing the conflict? Then, work them through the questions (listed earlier in this chapter), making sure to keep the ultimate goal, *working effectively together,* prominent in their minds.

Although it would be nice for all your direct reports to like each other, that is too much to expect. But you can expect them to work together effectively. Your job is to coach your people until they understand that respect is critical for the work to get done. That means they need to demonstrate respect, which often translates into understanding that people don't all show respect in the same way. When people understand that not everyone shows respect in the same way, behaviors that may have been seen as disrespectful are easier to shrug off. And when everyone feels they are respected—in the way they want to be respected—many, many conflicts will simply evaporate.

What You Should Have Learned from This Chapter

- People of all generations want respect; they just define it differently.
- People in positions of authority want their decisions to be respected.
- Older people want their experience and wisdom to be respected and deferred to.
- Younger people would like their fresh ideas and suggestions to be respected.
- Questions do not necessarily demonstrate disrespect.

| **Trust Matters**

Shortly after we began our research, we asked one young professional if he thought his organization would be interested in participating. He was very interested in the results, saying that he really wanted to know what the people in his organization thought about the topics and how his organization would compare with other organizations. But he declined, saying,

> We really can't—and I can't suggest that we do. The problem is that no one would fill out the survey. I know I wouldn't fill out the survey, because I would be concerned about what the organization would do with the information. I want the information, but I think that the administration would use that information to hurt me in some way. I don't know how they'd do it; I just don't trust them not to use information in the worst possible way. So it is better for me not to have my company participate.

One of the issues we've heard a lot about from people is how much less trust there is in today's workplace in comparison with the past. People from every generation and at every level tell us that employees, managers, and leaders don't trust each other anymore. They tell us that this lack of trust has a negative effect on organizations because they feel they have to spend more time covering themselves in case of future problems. They tell us they spend more time questioning what management is doing because they don't trust management to do the right thing. They tell us that because they trust so few people they work with, they spend less time being productive and actually getting the work done. Some of the complainers place the blame squarely on the shoulders of younger employees, saying that it is their lack of trust (which is often termed *cynicism*) in others that is causing the work world to suddenly become less than idyllic (as it presumably was before?).

> [The organization should have] trust that
> extends both up and down the hierarchy.
> —Silent

Others say that it's the older people who are at fault; they are jaded and don't trust the people in charge because they've had so much experience with organizations—they no longer *believe.*

> [Organizations should] treat their employees with respect and trust.
> —Early Xer

Still others blame the organizations; they believe that in the past, organizations had the best interests of their employees at heart. They suggest that when the organizations took care of their employees first, the employees trusted the organization, and everything worked better because everybody trusted everybody else.

What is the nature of trust in organizations today? Do people at work trust each other and the organizations they work for? Is there any difference in the level of trust by generation? Do people higher up in an organization trust more than do people at lower levels in the organization? And why does it matter whether someone doesn't trust his or her boss or organization?

> The organization should be trustworthy; not lie to the employees.
> —Early Boomer

Research

We looked for answers to these questions in the comments volunteered in response to the questions about career challenges, retention, and generational conflict, and in responses to the specific questions we asked about trust.

Do people at work trust each other and the organizations they work for? Is there any difference in the level of trust by generation?
We asked people to tell us whether they agreed with the following five statements:

1. I trust my peers at work.
2. I trust my direct reports.
3. I trust upper management to do the right thing.
4. I trust my current boss.
5. I trust my organization to keep its promises.

I Trust My Peers at Work. Overall, 61% of respondents said they trust their peers. But of course this means that 39% don't trust their peers—or that they are neutral, which is almost as negative. We say it is almost as negative to give a neutral response because—in the case of these items—saying you are neutral is actually a negative response. Think about it this way: if someone asks you if you trust them and you say you are neutral, are you actually saying you trust them? We find that when people say they are neutral, what they are really saying is that they don't trust whoever they are talking about, they just don't want to say so. There were no differences by generation, so trust (or lack thereof) in peers at work has nothing to do with what generation someone belongs to.

I Trust My Direct Reports. Only 7% of respondents said they didn't trust their direct reports; 64% said they did trust their direct reports. And 29% said they were neutral about whether they trusted their direct reports, which (as we explained earlier) is almost as bad as saying they don't trust them. There were no differences by generation.

I Trust Upper Management to Do the Right Thing. Overall, 47% of respondents said they trusted upper management to do the right thing. That means that 53% said they either didn't trust management or were neutral about whether they trusted management to do the right thing. There were no differences by generation.

I Trust My Current Boss. Overall, 70% of respondents said they trusted their current boss; responses didn't differ by generation. Research by Gallup has shown that an employee's relationship with his or her boss is one of the primary reasons people stay with or leave an organization.

I Trust My Organization to Keep Its Promises. Overall, 54% of respondents said they trusted their organization, which means that 46% did not trust their organization. There were no statistically significant differences by generation. However, there was a trend in the data such that those in the middle of their careers (Early Boomers, Late Boomers, and Early Xers) were less trusting of their organization than were those at the beginning and end of their careers (Silents and Late Xers; see Figure 3.1). Perhaps how much you trust an organization is more strongly influenced by how much you have to lose (where you are in your career) than it is by which generation you are from.

Overall, the results show that people of all generations are more trusting of specific people than they are of the organization they work for and of its upper management. Again, more than 60% of people say they trust their peers and direct reports, and 70% say they trust their boss, whereas only 54% say they trust their organization, and 47% say they trust upper management.

It is much easier to trust a particular person than it is to trust a group of people or an organization as a whole; after all, you know (or have some idea) of how an individual person is going to act, but you never know for sure how a group of people or a larger organization is going to act. Therefore, people of all generations are much more likely to trust specific people than they are groups of people.

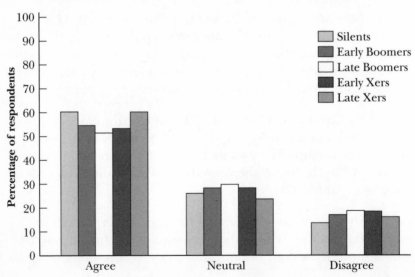

Figure 3.1. Responses to the Statement, "I Trust My Organization to Keep Its Promises," by Generation.

Male and Female Employees' Levels of Trust

In case you were wondering, in our data there are no significant differences in how much male and female employees trust their peers, their direct reports, their bosses, upper management, or the organization. Further, there are no differences among women of different generations or men of different generations. In other words, it doesn't matter if the female was born in the 1950s or the 1970s, she is equally likely to trust (or distrust) the people around her. The same is true for men.

"What's so new about all this? I've never trusted anyone over thirty, under thirty, or thirty."

Is lack of trust an issue of level in the organization rather than an issue of age? Do people higher in an organization have different levels of trust than do people at lower levels in the organization?
Going back to the five statements we asked people about, the research reveals the following:

I Trust My Peers at Work. There were no differences by level, indicating that trust (or lack thereof) in peers at work has nothing to do with level in an organization.

I Trust My Direct Reports. There were some differences by organizational level, with respondents at the top and executive level being more likely to say that they did trust their direct reports than were other managers or professionals.

I Trust Upper Management to Do the Right Thing. About 50%—of people at each level—trusted upper management. So apparently about half of the people don't trust upper management to do the right thing—even if they are members of upper management themselves!

I Trust My Current Boss. There were no differences by organizational level. Overall, 70% of people—at all levels—said they trusted their boss.

I Trust My Organization to Keep Its Promises. When you look at Figure 3.2, what is apparent is that more people at higher levels in organizations trust their organization than do people at lower levels. Specifically, more than 70% of people in the top and executive ranks said that they trusted their organization, while 56% of upper management did, 51% of management did, and 47% of professionals did. This result demonstrates that there is a significant difference between the level of trust people higher and lower in organizations have for their organizations. So is it any surprise that there is often a disconnect between the people who direct organizations and the people below them?

There are some differences in whom (and what) employees trust as a result of their level in the organization. Whether they trust (or distrust) their peers, boss, and upper management doesn't depend on their level in the organization. Interestingly, people at

Figure 3.2. Responses to the Statement, "I Trust My Organization to Keep Its Promises," by Organizational Level.

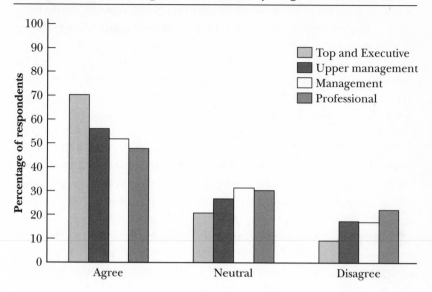

higher levels in organizations—such as the people who report to the CEO—are *not* more likely to say they trust their bosses than are people at lower levels.

Although trust in the boss does not increase as employees reach higher levels in the organization, trust in direct reports does. The higher employees are in the organization, the more likely they are to say they trust their direct reports.

Also, the higher employees are in the organization, the more likely they are to trust the organization as a whole. Specifically, C-level executives (CEO, CFO, CIO, or CTO, for example) and others in the executive ranks are more likely than everyone else is to say they trust their organization to keep its promises. Of course they trust the organization more—they're in control of what the organization is going to do! (Or at least they are more in control than are people at lower levels.)

> *Do not let deeds belie your words, lest when*
> *you speak in church someone may say to himself,*
> *"Why do you not practice what you preach?"*
> —SAINT JEROME (c. 342–420 A.D.)

It also makes sense that people at higher levels would complain that people lower in the organization don't trust the organization as much as they do. *They* trust the organization; why doesn't everybody else? Well, everybody else doesn't trust the organization because everybody else isn't in charge of it. Just as you trust an individual you know personally more than you do a group of people, you're more likely to trust an organization if you are one of the people who are in charge of making the decisions for that organization. After all, it is much easier to trust yourself to keep your promises to yourself than it is to trust other people to keep their promises to you!

Does it matter if someone doesn't trust his or her boss or organization?

Well, whether it matters depends in part on whether you care about retention. When we look at how much people trust their boss and their organization and then look at whether they say they are going to be with the organization in three years, what we find is that how much people say that they trust their boss (Figure 3.3) and their organization (Figure 3.4) affects whether they say they are going to stay with the organization.

Figure 3.3. Responses to the Statement, "I Trust My Current Boss" (Grouped According to Respondents' Plans for Staying with the Organization).

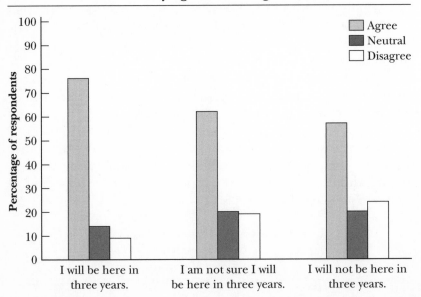

Trust is very important for retention. The people who either don't trust their organization or aren't sure if they trust their organization (which basically means they don't) are significantly more likely to say they are going to leave than are people who say that they do trust their organization.

Trust and Time

The amount of time employees have spent with their organization appears to have an effect on trust. What we find is that people who are new to an organization (who have been working there less than a year) trust their organization more than do employees who have been there longer than a year. However, they do not have more trust in their direct reports, their peers, their bosses, or upper management. So trust in a particular person (or particular group of people) does not change with tenure, but trust in an organization as a whole declines after the year-long "honeymoon."

Figure 3.4. Responses to the Statement, "I Trust My Organization to Keep Its Promises" (Grouped According to Respondents' Plans for Staying with the Organization).

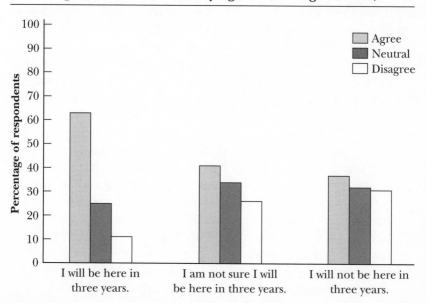

Trust Matters

Our research results clearly show that the different generations have similar levels of trust in their organization and in upper management—they don't trust them much. Fundamentally, the ability of an organization to function effectively rests almost entirely on the willingness of employees, managers, and executives to trust each other—to trust both that the work will get done and that the motives for decisions are at worst benign. If this willingness to trust is absent, an organization is much slower, less efficient, less viable, less pleasant to work for—and one you're looking to escape from.

The research suggests that trust (or the lack thereof) for an organization as a whole and for managers and leaders in particular has a serious impact on two major aspects of organizational health: retention and efficiency.

Never esteem anything as of advantage to you that will
make you break your word or lose your self-respect.
—MARCUS AURELIUS ANTONINUS, 121–180 A.D.

As we've shown, lack of trust in an organization (and in the people in the organization) has a direct (and negative) effect on retention of employees. People who do not trust their organization are more likely to say they are looking to leave. Replacing employees who leave voluntarily costs an organization money in lost time, search costs, training costs, and so on. Thus, in a very practical way, employees' lack of trust in an organization is quite expensive.

Lack of trust within organizations (and in the people in the organization) also renders the people in an organization considerably less efficient, as the following example shows.

> Amy (an Early Xer) reports to Sarah (an Early Boomer), whom Amy doesn't trust. (Amy jokes that if she and Sarah got out of a sinking ship with two life preservers, Amy would expect Sarah to use one, to keep the other as a spare, and to tell Amy she should look on staying afloat as a career challenge!) Amy knows that Sarah does not believe that Sarah has any obligation to her direct reports— Sarah's past behavior has clearly shown that. Amy knows that if anything in the department isn't done perfectly and someone comments, Sarah will blame Amy or one of Amy's peers—even if Sarah is the one at fault. Amy understands that her boss will hang her out to dry any time she feels a need to.

Amy doesn't attribute Sarah's behavior to her age; this is just who Sarah is. But Amy has heard Sarah use her greater age as a reason for why she's right and Amy is wrong. Amy has requested a transfer many times, but as of now the transfer hasn't come because of political issues within the division. Basically, the people who could transfer her think that Amy should just shut up and deal with it. Amy thinks her concerns aren't being taken seriously in part because she is younger.

Because Amy doesn't trust her boss and therefore feels she has to protect herself by documenting everything she does, she gets a lot less done than she could. She no longer communicates anything important by phone. She knows she has to have written proof in case her boss decides to change her mind at the last minute and blame Amy because the work is not done. Amy spends a lot of (in her mind, wasted) time talking with people in the division to find out what her boss may be thinking now and what Amy is likely to be blamed for soon. She believes that if her boss were honest and decent to her direct reports (and took responsibility for her own decisions), they would be much more efficient at work—as well as happier.

Unfortunately, Sarah is still there and is unlikely to leave because she is a highly political person who has "dirt" on all the people who could fire her. Amy feels stuck. She can't trust her boss, and the organization hasn't transferred her—and doesn't seem likely to. Because she isn't happy and doesn't see any likelihood of the issue's being fixed, she has decided that the only alternative to continuing to work in the current situation (which she hates) is to leave the organization. So Amy is looking for another job during work time. She figures she might as well be productive at something!

If Amy trusted her boss, she would spend less time trying to anticipate the boss's behavior and would be much more efficient. Amy has thought a lot about what causes Sarah to behave as she does, and has come to the conclusion that her boss just doesn't care about the people who work for her and doesn't even see any advantage to herself in helping the people who report to her. In Amy's opinion, Sarah has not learned one of the most basic management tenets: that direct reports, if well trained and well led, can multiply your productivity and make you look very, *very* good.

Sarah probably doesn't trust the people above her any more than she trusts the people below her. Sarah's time in organizations may have taught her that she will get farthest by thinking only about what is best for herself. She may be in over her head and unable to do a better job than she is currently. Just as one can't be sure of people's values from what they do (Principle 1), Amy can't be sure why Sarah acts as she does. And because Amy doesn't trust her boss, she certainly can't ask!

Given that Amy isn't going to be able to find out why her boss does what she does (and therefore how to fix the issue if it's fixable), what might Amy be able to do to improve her situation? She has several choices. One course of action would be for Amy to find a new job in another organization. She could also continue to try for a transfer within her organization. Another option might be to find someone she trusts and ask for some coaching (see Principle 10).

Asking for coaching from someone you trust is a good way to get really practical advice about what else you might do that you haven't already done. Sometimes people who see the situation from a different perspective can suggest options that didn't appear to you to be available.

Consider another example:

> Gary couldn't stand his boss, Susan. She drove him nuts. She was incessantly positive, happy in a fake way, and so bouncy it was annoying. Furthermore, she had a habit of asking her direct reports for suggestions about how to improve their division, but received any suggestions very badly. When Gary offered suggestions, Susan got angry and accused him of being negative and destructive to morale.
>
> Gary was fed up and had no idea of what to do to stop being annoyed— other than blowing up at Susan, which would be a career-limiting move.
>
> So Gary went to Karen (a colleague) to ask for ideas about how to deal with Susan's annoying behavior. Karen had a few suggestions:
>
> - Figure out why Susan is behaving as she is. Is it to be manipulative, or is she just needy?
> - What can you live with, and what can you not live with?
> - Given what you think she's like as a person, do you actually expect her to act on your suggestions? If not, and if it makes you angry when she doesn't act on them, don't keep making them!
> - Go to Susan's boss and ask for coaching on how to deal with these issues. By asking for coaching rather than making a complaint, you force Susan's boss to put himself in your shoes and think about the problem from your perspective. If the boss doesn't have a solution, then how can he expect you to? And perhaps then he'll see a reason to do what he can to fix the problem.

- In the end, if the atmosphere is seriously destructive to your health and happiness (beyond what is expected in any job!), you need to think about going elsewhere.

There are certain risks involved with any course of action, to be sure, but if we allow ourselves to step into Gary's world right about here, armed with what we now know about trust in the workplace, we would suggest the following:

Gary—and Amy from the prior example—should also consider carefully the merits of the job at hand and whether those merits factor in heavily enough to make some confrontation worthwhile. As Rob Galford, managing partner of the Center for Executive Development in Boston, likes to say, "Ask: Is the grief worth the relief?" In other words, is the payoff for fixing the problem actually worth the pain you are going to have to go through to fix the problem?

The Benefits of Trust

We've talked about how both retention and efficiency suffer in organizations in which people lack trust. Now consider the flip side. The presence of trust among employees and between employees and managers has many benefits.

Increased Efficiencies

Trust has tangible benefits to both individuals and organizations. For individuals of all generations, trust makes interacting easier and more positive (Young and Daniel, 2003). If you don't trust the people you're interacting with, you have to double-check everything they say. If you trust the people you work with, you spend less time doing that. If you don't trust the people you work with, you spend a lot of time watching for people stabbing you in the back and trying to trip you up. You spend less time doing that if you trust the people you work with. Although some employees do get a kick out of being able to overcome, work around, and avoid the people trying to cause them trouble, even these employees need someone in their organization whom they actually trust. To have nobody you can trust in the whole organization is wearing, and just takes a great deal of effort away from actually getting the work done.

For organizations, trust reduces transaction costs. If trust does not exist among at least some people in the organization—whatever their generation—the employees have to spend time figuring out whom they can trust and when and under what conditions they actually can trust them. This of course increases the time it takes to get work done (Kramer, 1999). When trust exists in an organization, the trust allows people to cooperate more freely. If people cooperate more freely, the organization becomes more efficient. In other words, there is less documentation and duplication of work because people are less concerned about having to cover their backsides. If people can go on and do their work without having to document it multiple times, they can be much more productive.

Voluntary Deference to Authority

Another way trust assists the organization is through what Kramer (1999) calls "voluntary deference in the hierarchical relationships." Voluntary deference is as much about having trust as it is about having respect. If you trust someone in authority, you're much more likely to voluntarily defer to their decisions—whether they are older or younger than you are. You presume that they are more likely to be right than wrong, and therefore you simply do what they tell you to do. You're less likely to feel the need to double-check what they are doing, try to figure out why they are doing it, and cover yourself just in case what they are doing is going to harm you. You trust them, so you don't feel the need to protect yourself.

Efficient organizational performance depends on employees' willingness to comply with the decisions of organizational authorities and on their voluntary compliance with their organization's rules and directives. Very efficient organizational performance depends on employees' trusting the hierarchy enough not to feel the need to cover for themselves by duplicating work or double-checking everything they're told to do.

How This Applies to You

What can you do to reestablish trust when it's gone? There's no surefire way, but we do offer a few things to think about if you find you don't trust someone you work with or feel that someone you work with doesn't trust you.

If you sense that a younger person doesn't trust you because you are older:

- Why do you think he doesn't trust you? Is it because he questions you? For many people, questioning is actually a sign of respect, not a sign of lack of trust. Is he questioning you because he thinks you're wrong or because he wants to understand and learn?
- What is really going on? Does she not trust you because of your age, or are you doing something that is causing her not to trust you? Are you saying one thing and then doing something else? Are you managing her too closely? Doing so will often make a person think that you don't trust her, so she won't trust you.
- Is it possible you're just being paranoid?

If you don't trust an older person because he or she is older:

- What is really going on? Is your lack of trust in him about his age? Is it about him as a person? Is it about how he manages? Is it about how well he does his job? Is it about how the organization is doing?
- Do you not trust her because you think she doesn't trust you? Are you being paranoid? Do you just think she is "past it"? If so, why? Is that a fair and accurate assessment of her as a person, or is it relevant only to one small part of what she does? Generally that kind of sweeping opinion is more applicable to one minor aspect of the person rather than to the whole individual.

If you sense that an older person doesn't trust you because you are younger:

- What is really going on? Does he not trust you because you are younger than he is (and therefore is presuming that you are less competent)? Has something specific happened to erode the trust? If so, what can you do to get others to feel that you are worthy of trust again? Can you ask them?
- Is it possible you're just being paranoid?

If you don't trust a younger person because he or she is younger:

- Do you think "Young people can't be trusted as much as older people can," or are you thinking "This young person can't be trusted"? If it is the former, is that what you thought when you were that age? Don't let yourself slide into the "but things are different now" trap—if you resented people for not trusting you when you were that age, why are you repeating the behavior? If it is the latter, then what is it about this person that is causing you not to trust her?
- Do you not trust him as a person? Do you believe that he is untrustworthy? For example, do you think he is sneaky and manipulative, with bad intentions? If so, why are you still working with him? Is it possible you are being paranoid? You should see if you can get away from this person if you think that he has bad intentions toward you. (Very few people fit into the "evil intentions" category.)
- Do you think she is not competent? If you think a younger person isn't competent, you need to ask yourself why you think that. Has she done something specific for which she was personally responsible that demonstrated to you that she is not competent? Or do you just think that people who are younger are, as a rule, less competent than people who are older? If that is what you believe, think back to what you thought when you were that age and to what you know people thought about you. You know what you didn't know then; what can you do now to help the younger person learn from your experience? Coaching her doesn't require you to trust her, but coaching her may help you understand when you can trust her.

If You Are a Manager

Remember that trust can't be bought with higher salaries or coaxed with better benefits; trust comes from deeper sources. Employees are likely to trust leaders who

- Do what they say they are going to do
- Are competent
- Look out for the employees' interests as well as their own
- Appear to care about the employees
- Explain why decisions are being made
- Really listen to the concerns of the employees

And what if you do something or something happens that results in losing your employee's trust? Some people appear to believe that they will increase employees' trust by

- Telling employees and colleagues what they want to hear
- Saying only positive things and denying that the negative realities of the situation are issues
- Pretending that everyone trusts them
- Acting as if they did nothing wrong in the past
- Acting hurt when someone says they aren't trustworthy
- Saying they did nothing wrong even while being indicted
- Generally behaving as if they are convinced by their own . . . verbiage

Whoever is telling executives to behave in these ways is partially right: if you pretend that nothing is wrong, some people will begin to question themselves and think that you must be trustworthy because you obviously don't think you've done anything wrong. Some employees and coworkers will believe the pretense and will trust you again. However, many people—especially the really street-smart ones—will not trust you again if you behave this way.

People are sometimes motivated to say what they know others want to hear, to tell half-truths, and to reassure with promises that *may* come true—if everything works out *exactly* as planned. Sometimes managers say things that aren't strictly accurate because they honestly believe everything will work out if people spend more time on the work and less time consumed with what might happen—and sometimes they're right. Sometimes they are just so tired of being in the middle of—and being blamed for—things they can't control that they just want the problem to go away, and that is understandable. Sometimes they think the problem isn't real, that it will go away if they can divert attention from it—and sometimes they're right. Sometimes they think that their people can't handle the truth, so they don't tell them.

Although such behavior is understandable and may be easier in the short run, it isn't going to accomplish your goals in the long run, nor is it ultimately in the best interest of the organization. Over time this behavior erodes credibility and often damages trust to the point that it can't be rebuilt.

Some people want to believe that it is acceptable to behave this way because trust can easily be reestablished. The truth is that trust is difficult to reestablish when it's gone. Think about personal relationships. Once trust is gone in a marriage or friendship, how easy is it to reestablish? Not very. It takes a long time and a lot of hard work. The same principle applies at work; once the trust is gone, it is difficult (if not nearly impossible) to bring it back. After all, when you hear someone say one thing and then see her do something that she said she was not doing (day after day for years), unless you are terminally naive you aren't just going to start believing what she tells you simply because she says she's telling the truth this time. "Fool me once, shame on you; fool me twice, shame on me" is a truism for a reason.

Now, having said all that, we're not saying you should volunteer the whole truth all the time. Telling 100% of the truth 100% of the time is as bad an idea as lying is. As Lucy Kellaway writes, "Sometimes painful things need to be said; but often true things are better left unsaid. The successful manager should be as economical with the truth as with the budget" (2005, p. 13). Not lying isn't the same thing as baring your soul. You need to balance being honest with holding back information that should not be provided. You also need to think about how you are going to withhold information you can't share, because often how the withholding of information is handled is at least as important as what is withheld. You need to keep in mind the possible short- and long-term implications of what you are saying and how you are saying it.

Although telling the whole truth may not always be the best policy, saying things you know to be untrue isn't a good idea either. Obviously this balancing act is easier to say than to do, especially when you're being put on the spot. Because not everyone is equally good at both being accurate and not saying too much, it is almost inevitable that trust breaks down at some point in nearly all organizations. Here are a few additional suggestions to help you avoid crossing that line accidentally.

- *Tell the truth—but don't feel you have to say everything you know or soften bad news with promises of a bright future. And if you can't tell the truth, say that you can't say anything.* It is always preferable (for the sake of maintaining trust) to tell the truth, but there are situations where an executive can't tell the complete truth for a variety of reasons. If you can't tell the truth, then tell the people asking that you can't say anything and that you don't want to lie to them.

Saying this might be more uncomfortable for you than a nice lie, but at least they won't think you're untrustworthy later on.

- *Don't use your level—or your age—as an excuse.* If someone lies and is caught in the lie, it doesn't matter what her level is in the organization: people aren't going to trust her anymore. Saying untrue things is not an executive perk, no matter what the big picture looks like and how much private information you have. You should hold yourself to the same standards of truth you expect others to uphold. (Depending on how cynical or realistic you are, you may be laughing out loud at this point. But among the top executives we've known—and we like to think it is also true in general—the executives most highly regarded for their integrity and honesty were also best able to lead their organizations.)

- *Change the bodies in the seats if you need to.* Sometimes you just have to replace people whom your employees don't trust with people they think are more trustworthy. Sometimes an individual has burned so many bridges that there is no way he is ever going to be

"Remember when I said I was going to be honest with you, Jeff? That was a big, fat lie."

trusted again (even if he denies ever playing with the matches!), and the only thing you can do to remedy the situation is to get rid of him.

Sometimes it is possible for a leader to repair the relationship and convince employees that they finally get how important trust is. Consider the following example:

Gary (a Late Boomer) was an executive who had been known for years at his company as someone who said one thing and meant another. He was well known to his direct reports of all ages for walking into meetings already knowing his decision, asking people for their opinion, and then getting angry with them when they offered an opinion different from the one he held but had not yet expressed. He was known for saying that his philosophy was one of participative, open leadership; however, his actual behavior was dictatorial, punishing, and micromanaging, and he would say whatever he wanted just to make things look good.

When others pointed out the discrepancy between what he said and what he did, he couldn't understand why people were having a problem; after all, he told them what his leadership philosophy was—what did it matter what he did? When the complaints came from people older than he was, he said it was because they were jealous and didn't like reporting to someone younger. When the complaints came from people younger than he was, he said they didn't know enough to complain and obviously had a personal problem. When the complaints came from someone his own age, he said they either were jealous or didn't understand what leading really was about. After all, what he *said* was important to him mattered more than what he *did,* right?

He finally received feedback from people his own age, as well as from people who were both older and younger than he was, about this pattern of behavior. These were people he couldn't ignore or discount. This feedback caused him to realize that people of all ages and levels in the organization didn't trust him because they saw a discrepancy between what he said and what he did. He finally understood that consistency between words and deeds was more important to the people who worked for him than his philosophy was. He finally realized that he couldn't say one thing and do something else and expect people to overlook the discrepancy or to accept what he was doing as reflecting his philosophy when it obviously wasn't. He could no longer blame the lack of trust in him on an age issue or on people's not understanding what it meant to be a leader.

Since he received the feedback, Gary has been working to change his behavior. He has been making a concerted effort to ensure that what he does is
consistent with what he says. He no longer punishes people for having alternative opinions and even occasionally asks for their opinions to be expressed.
People have noticed the differences but are hesitant to believe that Gary's new
behavior will last; after all, a leopard doesn't change its spots.

Sometimes there isn't much you can do except tell the truth
over and over again and hope that eventually people will finally
start believing you again. In Gary's case, it did work. In the year
since we first heard his story, Gary has done an excellent job of
reestablishing trust with people in his organization. The people he
works with report that Gary behaves as if he is honestly interested
in alternative opinions. He frequently asks for feedback about his
behavior from people of all ages and levels. Gary's behavior is now
seen as being consistent with what he says; in other words, he is finally "walking his talk." People really do think that the leopard's
spots have changed dramatically. With enough effort, change that
results in renewed trust can be accomplished!

What You Should Have Learned from This Chapter

- People of all generations and at all levels are more likely to
  trust the people they work with directly (bosses, peers, and
  direct reports).
- People trust their organizations less than they do the people
  they work with directly.
- People trust upper management less than they trust their
  organization.
- What generation you are from or how old you are does not
  affect how much you trust other people or your organization.
- The less people trust, the more likely they are to leave.

People Want Leaders Who Are Credible and Trustworthy

People are affected by the culture from which they came. Earlier generations were more accustomed to authoritarian types of leadership while the younger generations need much looser reigns [sic].
—Late Boomer

Everyone has an idea of what attributes a leader should have. But not everyone has the same idea. One of the concerns we hear most often is that there is a major disconnect among the generations with regard to ideas about and attitudes toward leadership. Office scuttlebutt is that the older generations want a command-and-control type of leader and that younger generations want leaders who include them in the making of every decision. Sometimes the failure of a leader is attributed to her not having the leadership attributes that one generation—or another—thinks are most necessary to be a good leader. Some leaders, people say, fail because they cannot "connect" with a particular generation of employees, not because they aren't "good leaders."

Just from reading the previous chapters (in particular, the preceding one on trust), you may already have a sense of what our research revealed about leadership. But read on! And consider the following example:

There was going to be a reduction in force (RIF) in a midsize technology company. Because he was an executive at the company, Sam knew that it was happening and knew who was going to be affected, but because of his position, he couldn't tell anyone what was going to happen. One day Jon (one of the people who was going to be let go and who was also Sam's friend) asked Sam specifically whether he was at risk. Sam looked Jon in the eye and said that he was not at risk in the RIF and that he shouldn't worry about it. Sam said that, knowing full well that Jon was going to lose his job in three weeks. When asked about it later (when it came out that he had known about it and had lied), Sam said he had no other choice because he had been told by his boss not to say anything. When asked why he couldn't have refused to answer or said something that was less of a direct lie, Sam said that to do so would've tipped Jon off because everyone knew that the layoffs were coming and that Sam knew the details, so he had to lie directly.

Did Sam behave as a good leader? The answer probably depends on whom you ask, and it definitely depends on what people expect of their leaders.

Many people talk about differences between older and younger people in terms of the attributes they desire and expect in their leaders, as if these differences were established facts. We heard people say these sorts of things so often—and express deep concerns about what they weren't doing to meet their employee's expectations—that when we started doing this research we set up a section just about leader attributes. People seem to agree that what younger and older people want from leaders is fundamentally different in critical ways. It's an interesting idea . . . but is it actually true? And if it is true, how and where do the generations differ in what they want from their leaders? If it isn't true, why do people think there are differences? These are the questions we asked going into our study.

Research

To evaluate what attributes people want in their leaders, we set up (as we did to research values) a computer program that presented people with 40 attributes of leaders in such a way that they had to prioritize some attributes over others.

After this process, each individual ended up with a list of ten attributes of leaders that he or she had chosen over the thirty other attributes. Using these top ten lists, we were then able to identify the leadership attributes that people said were most important for their leaders to have. We were also able to isolate the attributes that people thought were least important for a leader to have—which ones were least likely to be kept throughout the prioritization process. And we were able to sort and compare these results by the age of the individuals participating and by their level in the organization.

Preferred Leadership Attributes

The leadership attributes chosen in the top ten most frequently were

CREDIBLE (69%)

TRUSTED (59%)

LISTENS WELL (55%)

FARSIGHTED (52%)

ENCOURAGING (50%)

DEPENDABLE (48%)

FOCUSED (44%)

A GOOD COACH (40%)

DEDICATED (38%)

EXPERIENCED (38%)

Of these attributes, CREDIBLE, TRUSTED, LISTENS WELL, FARSIGHTED, and ENCOURAGING were chosen by more than 50% of the people surveyed. Although there is agreement in what people want in their leaders, the most striking characteristic of these data is that the responses are spread out among the choices.

Do people from different generations want their leaders to have different attributes?

When you look at all 40 attributes that people could choose from, it is clear that the generations are quite similar in what attributes they want in their leaders. (See Appendices C and D for the complete list of attributes and the percentage of respondents in each generation who placed the attributes in their top ten.)

For example, given conventional wisdom, you might expect that older people would focus more on experience as an important attribute in a leader than younger people do. Contrary to this expectation, we found that the attribute EXPERIENCED is not chosen much more frequently by Silents and Early Boomers than it is by Early and Late Xers. Therefore, it isn't accurate to say that older generations are more focused on experience as an attribute for a leader than are younger generations; younger generations think that experience is as important in a leader as older generations do.

Similarly, given conventional wisdom, you might expect that younger people would focus on a leader as a coach more often than older people would. Contrary to this expectation, we found that A GOOD COACH is not chosen much more often by Early Xers than it is by Early or Late Boomers; in fact, Late Boomers choose this attribute more often than Early and Late Xers do.

Different from the other generations, Silents included DELEGATING in their top ten leadership attributes, and Early Boomers included CREATIVE. Early Boomers, Late Boomers, and Early Xers included PERSUASIVE as one of their top ten attributes. Late Xers included OPTIMISTIC and TRUSTING, which the other generations did not.

All generations listed CREDIBLE, TRUSTED, LISTENS WELL, ENCOURAGING, and DEPENDABLE in their top 10, and most people included FARSIGHTED, FOCUSED, A GOOD COACH, DEDICATED, and EXPERIENCED (see Table 4.1).

Least Frequently Chosen Leadership Attributes

The leadership attributes GLOBAL LEADERSHIP IMAGE, GLOBALLY INNOVATIVE, HAS A GLOBAL VIEW, INTERNATIONALLY RESILIENT, GOOD FUND-RAISER, PHYSICALLY FIT, and WHOLESOME were chosen in the top ten less than 10% of the time. Many of the least frequently chosen attributes focused more on the global aspects of leadership and on what is required of a leader in an organization that does business outside of the United States. It appears that few participants believe it is critical for leaders in their organizations to do a good job in fund-raising, to be wholesome, or to be physically fit. Though few believe that being physically fit is an important attribute for a leader to have, there are data to suggest that being in good physical condition actually does help a good leader perform better—even if others don't see it as being particularly important (McDowell-Larsen, Campbell, and Kearney, 2002).

Table 4.1. Top Ten Leadership Attributes, by Generation (including percentage of respondents selecting each attribute).

Silents	Early Boomers	Late Boomers	Early Xers	Late Xers
CREDIBLE 65%	CREDIBLE 74%	CREDIBLE 75%	CREDIBLE 71%	LISTENS WELL 68%
LISTENS WELL 59%	TRUSTED 61%	TRUSTED 60%	TRUSTED 58%	DEPENDABLE 66%
TRUSTED 59%	FARSIGHTED 57%	FARSIGHTED 59%	FARSIGHTED 54%	DEDICATED 63%
FARSIGHTED 53%	LISTENS WELL 55%	LISTENS WELL 53%	LISTENS WELL 51%	FOCUSED 59%
DELEGATING 50%	ENCOURAGING 50%	ENCOURAGING 53%	ENCOURAGING 46%	TRUSTED 56%
ENCOURAGING 44%	FOCUSED 39%	DEPENDABLE 49%	DEPENDABLE 46%	ENCOURAGING 54%
DEPENDABLE 41%	DEPENDABLE 38%	A GOOD COACH 46%	FOCUSED 43%	CREDIBLE 48%
DEDICATED 38%	PERSUASIVE 34%	FOCUSED 44%	A GOOD COACH 40%	OPTIMISTIC 45%
EXPERIENCED 38%	A GOOD COACH 33%	EXPERIENCED 41%	EXPERIENCED 36%	EXPERIENCED 43%
A GOOD COACH 38%	CREATIVE 33%	PERSUASIVE 37%	PERCEPTIVE 35%	TRUSTING 40%

The overall message is that there are more similarities among the generations in what attributes they want in a leader than there are differences. But what about people at different levels in the organization? Do people at different levels want different attributes in their leaders?

Do people at different levels in organizations say they want different things from their leaders?

Overall, people in the top and executive, upper management, management, and professional ranks want the same attributes in their leaders (CREDIBLE, FARSIGHTED, TRUSTED, A GOOD COACH). However, there were a few interesting differences between people at different levels on which attributes are most important.

Though CREDIBLE and DEPENDABLE showed up as important leadership attributes for people at all levels, they were chosen less frequently by people in the top and executive ranks of organizations than by people at the three lower levels. (See Table 4.2 and Appendix E for the percentages of respondents at different organizational levels who placed particular leader attributes in their top ten.) This difference is particularly interesting given the issues with trust in an organization. One explanation for this difference is that people at lower levels don't trust upper management and would like them to be more dependable, whereas people in the top and executive ranks don't consider being dependable as important as being persuasive, farsighted, or focused.

A similar pattern is apparent for the attribute ENCOURAGING. Though it showed up frequently for people at all levels, it was chosen less often by people in the top and executive ranks of organizations than it was by people at the three lower levels. Apparently people in the top and executive ranks think it is less important for leaders to be encouraging than people at lower levels in the organization think it is. Does that mean that people at lower levels are being more encouraging than people at higher levels, or that everyone wants his or her boss to be encouraging, but the people at the highest level just don't think it is that important?

People at the higher levels of organizations (top and executive and upper management) included PERSUASIVE in their top ten more frequently than did management and professional-level

Table 4.2. Top Ten Leadership Attributes, by Organizational Level (including percentage of respondents selecting each attribute).

Top/Executive	Upper Management	Management	Professional
CREDIBLE 68%	CREDIBLE 74%	CREDIBLE 75%	CREDIBLE 77%
FARSIGHTED 66%	FARSIGHTED 58%	TRUSTED 61%	LISTENS WELL 58%
TRUSTED 58%	TRUSTED 55%	LISTENS WELL 51%	TRUSTED 57%
LISTENS WELL 53%	LISTENS WELL 48%	ENCOURAGING 51%	FARSIGHTED 57%
FOCUSED 51%	ENCOURAGING 48%	DEPENDABLE 51%	ENCOURAGING 48%
PERSUASIVE 45%	DEPENDABLE 46%	FARSIGHTED 48%	DEPENDABLE 43%
DEDICATED 44%	EXPERIENCED 41%	FOCUSED 42%	FOCUSED 43%
ENCOURAGING 42%	A GOOD COACH 39%	A GOOD COACH 41%	PERCEPTIVE 42%
A GOOD COACH 39%	FOCUSED 38%	DEDICATED 39%	A GOOD COACH 40%
DEPENDABLE 36%	PERSUASIVE 37%	A GOOD TEACHER 36%	EXPERIENCED 37%

people. It makes sense that people at higher levels in the organization would be more likely to consider this attribute a high priority more frequently than do people at lower levels in the organization: the higher you go in an organization, the more that your work entails persuading others to agree to carry out your plans.

People Want Leaders Who Are Credible and Trustworthy

People of different generations agree on what attributes their leaders should have. People of all generations and at all levels want their leaders to be credible, farsighted, encouraging, dependable, and trustworthy, and to listen well. Perhaps if everyone knows that this is what everyone wants, it will be easier for leaders to behave this way!

Author's Riff

So, people want their leaders to be credible, trusted, and dependable. Are these the attributes of individuals who rise into positions of leadership in organizations and in our political life? Or are these positions filled only by people driven by a desire for the power and status that comes from making it to the top? Perhaps the people who make it to the top do so because they want power, and for them to be perceived as a good leader they have to be able to fake dependability and authenticity so that their people will think them credible and trustworthy.

Occasionally, though, you find exceptional leaders who you know have been driven to make it to the top because they believe they can do more good from there than from lower down. Perhaps they are few and far between, but they do exist. (Maybe we just don't hear about them as much because they don't make for provocative news.) What we do know is this: they are amazing to work for! Jim Collins's book *Good to Great* provides more than a glimpse of some of these people; we recommend you read it.

How This Applies to You

Just because you don't supervise someone doesn't mean you're not a leader in your organization. Many different people in organizations are leaders—and not all of them are in positions of formal authority. If you think about it, you'll be able to name people who are leaders in your organization because of some combination of their personal clout, experience, reputation, and insight. Their lack of formal authority doesn't make them not leaders. So regardless of your formal position in the organization, you do need to think about the advice for leaders.

Our best advice (in part based on the research, and in part from our collective experience): You won't go far wrong if you behave as you would like your leaders to behave. Do you want your leaders to be credible? You should be credible. Do you want them to be dependable? You should be dependable. Do you want them to be encouraging? You should be encouraging. And so on.

You need to be as you want others to be. You cannot change others' behavior (no matter how much you might want to or how right you would be!); the only person's behavior you can change is your own. And if you want one of those leadership positions that come with organizational authority, it would be a good idea to start practicing now how you want to be as a leader.

If You Are a Manager

Lack of confidence in leaders isn't about a generational disagreement about what a leader should be; it is about what leaders are *doing* to show they are good leaders. Unfortunately it is difficult for anyone to be all things to all people—and especially to people of all generations and all levels in the organization simultaneously. Even when *credible* is explicitly defined as "believable, ethical, trustworthy; has few hidden motives," what does the person have to do to be seen as credible by any specific individual? We know that people want the same attributes in their leaders; what we don't know is what leaders need to do to be identified that way by everyone.

Speaking of credibility, let's return to the example about Sam and Jon that we had mentioned earlier. In the future, would you consider Sam credible? Was Sam's behavior as a leader in his organization ethical? Has Sam shown himself to be dependable? How about trustworthy? Would you believe his word if he told you something in his capacity as your manager? Or would you wonder what was really going on, and wait for the whole story to come out?

Well, what you would do probably depends on your position. If you're Sam's boss, you think he is highly trustworthy and dependable. Sam put his obligation to his boss and the organization ahead of his obligation to his friend Jon and ahead of not lying as a principle. If you are in Jon's position, you are likely to think that Sam isn't trustworthy or ethical because he lied directly to someone who asked him a direct question. Worse, Jon had a personal relationship with Sam; if Sam would lie about this sort of thing to Jon, you might wonder (and you probably know) what he would do to everyone else.

What about the future? Suppose that someday Sam ends up as his boss's colleague—a division or department head with equal standing. Because Sam's boss knows that Sam lied directly to Jon, is Sam's boss going to trust him? Or is he going to think that Sam is trustworthy because he knows that Sam's first loyalty is to the organization, not to the people around him? Different people will have different answers.

In this case, Jon and Sam were friends, but Jon did not report to Sam. Sam had thoroughly discussed the pending RIF with his boss (from whom he received the information), and had been told directly that he could not divulge the information to anyone under any circumstances.

What was Sam to do? He was stuck. He had received a direct order that he couldn't tell anyone what was happening. To do so could have compromised his career. At the same time, he was asked a direct question by someone he considered to be a friend. His lying to Jon ended his friendship, compromised his credibility with the people who knew he had lied, and potentially hurt his friend financially as well as emotionally—even though he wasn't personally responsible for any decision other than not telling Jon what was going to happen.

In fact, Sam could've said that he hadn't heard anything. That would still be lying to Jon, but it was actually the lie that was required by the instructions he had been given by his boss. Sam violated those instructions by saying anything at all.

Another option for Sam would've been to tell Jon that he (Sam) had been told that he couldn't tell anyone what was going to happen. That would've been the most direct and honest answer Sam could've given Jon. Jon would not necessarily have been happy with that answer, but at least Sam wouldn't have been lying to him.

It would be nice if we could tell you that there was a simple, right, and most moral answer to Sam's dilemma. But as far as we can tell, there isn't one. Sam had an obligation to his friend Jon. Sam had an obligation to his boss and to the organization. And Sam had an obligation to his family not to put his own career in jeopardy. Every individual leader has to decide which obligations to put first—and then has to live with the consequences of those decisions.

The easiest piece of advice to give is to Jon, not Sam. Jon should have known that he'd be putting Sam in a bind by asking him about the RIF, and he could have chosen not to ask Sam the question. We understand that in real life, it would be very difficult for Jon to not try to get any information about his future. But Jon needs to remember that he put Sam in a bad position by asking the question, and we hope that in time, Jon understands the very real struggle Sam had in the second before he had to respond to Jon's question.

How you decide if someone is credible or dependable or trustworthy is contingent both on what the person does and on your position within the organization, because how one part of the organization defines what is dependable and trustworthy behavior is not necessarily how another would. As you can see, often in these cases, where you stand depends on where you sit.

Does Age Matter at All?

As the research indicates, age does not appear to matter much. People of all generations want their leaders to be credible, to be trusted, to listen well, to be farsighted, and to be encouraging. A couple of fine points also are worth considering.

- It is a good idea to make sure younger employees feel listened to. They want to be heard and are likely to feel that they aren't.

- When working with older employees, it is a good idea to emphasize your experience. They understand and appreciate the experience people bring to the table and expect you to appreciate theirs.

We've just made some age distinctions, but remember that people of *all* generations want these behaviors from their leaders; some generations just may need it less (or more) frequently than others. Luckily that means you don't have to radically change your leadership style for every generation you encounter; as long as you are credible, are farsighted with regard to the business, listen well to the people around you, generate trust, and are encouraging of your employees, you'll do fine with people of all generations. That's in addition to making good business decisions, of course!

What You Should Have Learned from This Chapter

- People of all generations and at all levels want their leaders to be credible, trustworthy, dependable, farsighted, encouraging, and good listeners.
- If you can't tell the truth, say that you can't talk about the subject; if possible, do not engage to begin with. Don't mislead intentionally.
- Behave as someone you would want to follow.
- If you work at having the attributes people want in a leader, you may lose out to the dissembling backstabbers, or you may end up on top . . . but at least you'll be less likely to end up in a defendant's chair!

Organizational Politics Is a Problem—No Matter How Old (or Young) You Are

Office politics plays a part in all organizations. So what is office politics? To some people, office politics is using persuasion and alliances to be successful at work. To others it is backstabbing, doing lunch, kissing up, and taking credit for other people's work. Whatever you think office politics is, what is certain is that it is inescapable as long as people work in groups of any size. But are there really some age groups who thrive on politics and others who do not? People have told us that Baby Boomers are the real stars of the political world within organizations, that Boomers like nothing better than working the system politically and beating the people around them. That's the reason they always want meetings and teams and are so focused on face time! We have also heard that one real difference between Gen Xers and earlier generations is how much Xers hate office politics.

Well, our research shows that those notions are bunk. It doesn't matter what generation you are. The truth is that everyone who isn't winning at the political game dislikes it!

Let's look at a typical situation in many organizations. A senior employee (Senior) leads large (read: visible and important) projects while mentoring the junior employee (Junior), who is leading a smaller and less prominent project. This way Senior is happy that she is getting credit for a valuable project, and Junior is happy because he is leading a project and gets to learn.

Political problems arise when business realities (for example, timelines, resources, and business priorities) up-end this structure. In a typical case, a change in business priorities causes one of the small projects (led by Junior) to grow in scope and visibility, and the large project (led by Senior) to be reduced in importance and size. So Junior's project is now beyond his current level of skill, and he needs to lean on Senior to get the work done. But Senior has her own project to worry about and has no personal stake in the other project, so does not make herself available to provide more help to Junior. Worse, sometimes the reduction in priority of Senior's project results in her being asked to work as a "resource" under Junior on Junior's project. That is where the political problems really begin.

When the priority of the projects changes, management doesn't want to reassign the project because of the political implications. Junior would consider it to be a slap in the face for the project to be taken away and given to Senior at that time. Unfortunately, Senior is unhappy not to be given the project now that it is obviously beyond the ability of Junior, and considers it to be a slap in the face to be asked to work under Junior. But management thinks that Senior should be mature enough to be willing to work under Junior temporarily for the good of the project and to help Junior develop more quickly.

There are a couple of problems with that assumption on the part of management. First, to be put under someone who is significantly your junior even for one project is not a comfortable situation for anyone involved. Second, it isn't always in the best interests of Senior to help Junior develop; after all, the more Junior knows, the more competition he is for Senior.

One outcome is that Senior doesn't help Junior as much as he needs, thus causing the project to stall or (worse) fail. Senior's presumption is that management will see that Junior can't do the work, and will reassign the project before it fails. If that doesn't happen, Senior's assumption is that management will learn from the failure and will reassign projects of that magnitude to Seniors, rather than leaving them with Juniors.

This situation is obviously a political one. Senior's presumption is that Junior is getting to keep the project for political reasons rather than because he is going to do as good a job as Senior would. And the presumption is mostly accurate. Management's presumption is that Senior will ignore the political implications of the situation and will do her best to make sure the work gets done. Often that doesn't happen because helping isn't necessarily in the individual best interest of Senior—and she knows it.

What management may forget (or decide to ignore) is that a perceived hierarchy based on experience, knowledge, and tenure still exists and is important—especially in a flat organizational structure. That means that the political implications of such a situation are also understood to be important by the people involved, and the ramifications are potentially catastrophic for the completion of the project.

Do these political problems actually arise more now than they did in the past, or is it that people now are under the impression that politics should have less of an impact on promotion, recognition, and pay than it actually does? Is politics becoming progressively more important as positional authority is eroded because organizations are moving to flatter organizational structures? Is it perhaps that, in the past, organizational politics was an accepted part of life, whereas now it is seen as a dirty little secret that really shouldn't exist because people should be rewarded based on their performance rather than on their skill at office politics?

It isn't clear if organizational politics is more important now than it used to be, but we do know that it is a point of conflict between the generations, as the case of Senior and Junior demonstrates. People from all generations are concerned about the effects of organizational politics on their careers, on being recognized for the work they are doing, and for getting access to the resources they need to do their job.

It probably won't come as a surprise to you if we say that employees don't think that people get ahead in organizations solely because of hard work and competence. Some (cynical? realistic?) employees believe that hard work and competence are the least important aspects of getting ahead—or at least that these attributes are less important than seniority, kissing up, "putting in your time," knowing somebody in the right place at the right time, and so on.

Now why would others' being promoted for reasons other than competence bother people enough for them to comment about it in response to different questions that weren't asking about political behavior? (This is a rhetorical question—we presume you know the answer, but just in case . . .) Well, what are people being told about how they are going to be promoted? Are they told, "Just do a good job and keep your head down, and you'll be promoted"? Or are they told that how they act politically within their organization is just as important as getting the job done? (Typically this message is implicit rather than explicit and is therefore missed by large numbers of people.)

Our experience is that people are generally *told* that it is more important to do a good job than it is to be skilled in office politics. But that's not true—and most people in organizations understand that politics is a factor, even if they don't like it. The questions, then, boil down to these: How important do people think organizational politics is in the workplace? What impact does organizational politics have? Do people think they get ahead because of performance, or because of organizational politics? How can people best navigate the political landscapes of their organizations, whatever their age or experience? How can they best understand their colleagues' and bosses' approaches to politics and work effectively within those contexts?

GREGORY

"I'd like your honest, unbiased and possibly career-ending opinion on something."

Research

We looked for answers to these questions in the comments about political behavior at work that were volunteered in response to the questions about career challenges, retention, and generational conflict, and in response to specific questions we asked about how people get ahead at work.

How important do you think internal politics is in your workplace? According to the people of all generations who filled out the survey, internal politics is one of the major issues that—believe it or not—actually interferes with getting their job done. For example, people wrote about how dealing with a bad boss, peer jealousy, political sabotage, managing older bosses, being the youngest one on an executive team, having political battles for resources, not being skilled politically, and not getting recognition for good work reduced their productivity significantly, causing them to get much less done for the good of the organization than they could. They also commented that sometimes the amount of "politicking" made them less energized to get anything done at all. In essence they said that politics made work much less interesting and much less fun, which caused them to do less and to want to do less.

Learning How to Be Political

Early Xers talked about needing to learn how to be more politically aware and savvy. They talked about how they thought it was a skill set they didn't have and one that they felt was important to learn. They understood the importance of political skills for doing well in an organization, although they obviously weren't happy about its appearing to be more important than doing the work well.

> Politics seems to be the primary driver for promotion (who you know with a vote) rather than one's performance record.
> —Early Xer

Politics Causing Bad Business Decisions

Another political issue that both Boomers and Xers talked about as having a significantly negative effect on getting their job done was that of political considerations getting in the way of what is best for the business. They said they thought it was bad for their organization when people were promoted because they were more politically suave, but it was even worse when decisions were made for political reasons that were obviously bad for business. They said it was obvious that some of the time people are thinking more about the political implications of a specific decision than about the business implications. The respondents understood that the political implications of decisions were important, but they thought it was bad business to pay less attention to the business implications of politically driven decisions.

This was especially of concern when it came to questions of resource allocation. People of all generations talked about how they saw resources being allocated as much because of political maneuvering as because of actual need. Some talked about how it angered and disgusted them that more thought wasn't being put into allocating resources according to what would make the business more productive rather than according to who had the most political acumen.

> Trying to balance corporate politics with
> what's right for the business objectives.
> —Early Xer, writing about one of her largest career challenges

Conflict—But Not About Politics

Contradicting the stereotype, only seven people talked about corporate politics as being a major point of conflict between generations— and people from all generations were represented in those seven responses. That is, a few people see differences between the generations with regard to organizational politics, but very few thought it was a critical issue.

Politics—Reality of Organizational Life

Aside from how they felt about organizational politics and its effects, many respondents—respondents of all generations—seemed to be resigned to the reality that organizational politics was a central part of the work that could neither be avoided nor eliminated.

> Forced to play the politics versus focusing on getting things
> achieved in the most efficient and effective manner.
> —Late Boomer, writing about one of his largest career challenges

Many of the comments about learning how to be better at organizational politics talked about how organizational politics was a standard (and potentially important) part of the job. People indicated that they were interested in improving their political skills because they thought it would help move their careers forward, increase their budgets, get them the right people resources, and get more attention for the good work they do. There was general understanding that political skills are a critical component in being able to move up in an organization and being effective at higher levels of management.

Politics and Retention

A few people (who spanned the age range of people surveyed) commented about how the political issues on the job were likely to make them leave their organization. Some said the ethical issues that came up because of office politics were enough to make them want to leave the organization unless the unethical behavior was stopped and the political behavior curbed. Others said they were likely to leave if the organization didn't start rewarding them as much as other people who weren't contributing as much to the organization but who were better at managing office politics.

> Recognize contributors over those who contribute less
> but are better at managing the political landscape.
> —Late Boomer, talking about what his organization
> needs to do to retain him as a committed employee

Politics and Promotion

Early and Late Boomers and Early Xers were particularly bothered by what appears to them to be a prioritization of politics over competence in promotions. They said it was often obvious that people were being promoted for political reasons rather than because they were good at their jobs. They said they didn't mind if people who were competent *and* very politically adept were promoted;

what bothered them was when people who were demonstrably less competent and productive than others were promoted because they were better at schmoozing with the bosses. Yes, they understood the importance of being politically adept, but should it really be prioritized above doing a good job? Respondents said it appeared as if those deciding on promotions actually thought it more important for employees to know how to effectively promote what they were doing in the organization than it was for them to actually be productive.

Integrity is like oxygen—the higher you go, the less there is of it.
—PETE GAGE

Many people commented about how often they felt discouraged and how often they questioned the ethics of the people involved in promotion decisions that appeared to reward political behavior more than productivity and competence. They said they sometimes thought that the decisions made for political reasons were not ethical. Some suggested that they were less interested in moving up in their organization because they felt that being at a higher level would require them to do things they considered to be unethical. Specifically, some said that to move up in an organization, they would have to be willing to make real ethical sacrifices. Both Xers and Boomers were concerned about this issue, and indicated that it was a significant demotivating factor for them.

I am uncomfortable with what I consider to be a lack of
ethical/professional standards demonstrated with the office
politics played by some of the executives in this company.
—Early Boomer

Do people think skill at office politics trumps performance?
This perspective was echoed in another part of the survey. We asked people to say how much they agreed with two statements: (1) "People in my organization get ahead because of their skill at office politics" and (2) "People in my organization get ahead because of how they perform." What we found is that 53% of respondents believe that people get ahead because of performance and that 44% believe that people get ahead because of their skill at office politics.

So overall, people thought that employees were being rewarded almost as much for office politics as they were for performance. Which leads us to this question: Did people of all generations believe this equally?

Listening to comments people make, you might think that younger people are more cynical and think office politics is more important than performance, whereas older people think that performance is more important than office politics because that's the environment they grew up in.

Alternatively, you might think that older people have learned through experience that office politics is more important than performance, whereas younger people, who have less experience, have bought the "competence counts" argument hook, line, and sinker and haven't been in organizations long enough to learn that politics is actually more important.

As illustrated in Figure 5.1, what we found is that people of all generations agreed to roughly the same extent that people get ahead because of how they perform. More than 50% of both older and younger generations agree with this statement—there isn't a

Figure 5.1. Responses to the Statement, "In My Company, People Get Ahead Based on Performance," by Generation.

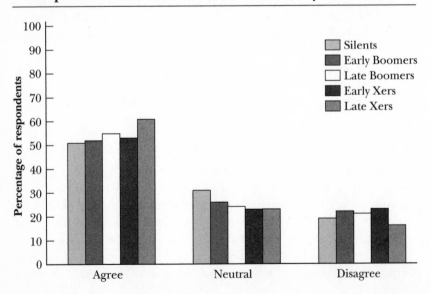

major difference as a function of either age or number of years with the organization.

The only small difference is that the youngest group—the Late Xers—is more likely than the other groups to say that people get ahead because of their performance. This result is consistent with the idea that younger people might be more likely to believe that hard work results in promotion because they have recently come from the educational system, where evaluations are based on more explicit criteria than those in the workplace, and they haven't been in the workplace long enough to see that this isn't always so.

However, there is a significant difference between generations with regard to the question of whether or not people advance because of their skill at office politics (see Figure 5.2).

Late Boomers and Early Xers are significantly more likely to agree with the statement, "People get ahead because of their skill at office politics," than are Silents, Early Boomers, and Late Xers. Late Xers agree less with this statement than even Silents do, and are more likely to be neutral than any other generation. These results suggest that younger people think that people get ahead because of

Figure 5.2. Responses to the Statement, "In My Company, People Get Ahead Because of Their Skill at Office Politics," by Generation.

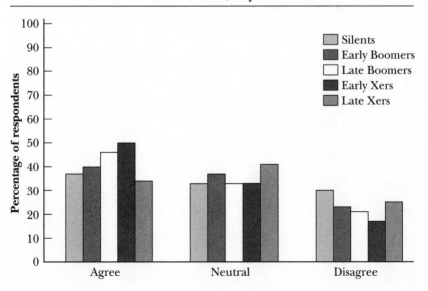

their skill in office politics more than older people do—once the younger people have had enough time in the workplace to identify the discrepancies that exist between performance and who gets promoted. But the pattern isn't a clear one, so perhaps there is another factor that can better explain the differences in perspectives.

What about organizational level? Do people at different levels in organizations have different opinions about why people get ahead?

Drum roll please . . . people who are higher in an organization believe that people get ahead because of how they perform rather than because of their skill at office politics. (Are you surprised?) Figures 5.3 and 5.4 show the survey results.

Conversely, employees lower in an organization think that people get ahead because of their skill at office politics, not because of how they perform.

It is apparent that there is a disconnect between how people higher and lower in organizations think people rise within organizations (surprised?). People higher in organizations attribute

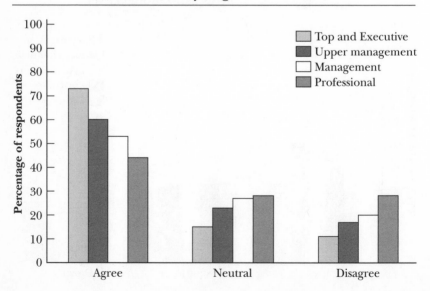

Figure 5.3. Responses to the Statement, "In My Company, People Get Ahead Based on Performance," by Organizational Level.

their own success to hard work and performance rather than to skill at office politics—whatever the truth of the matter. Have you ever heard someone at the top of an organization say he got there because he was a friend of the top guy or because he was good at making himself look good? Probably not.

On the flip side, people lower in organizations attribute others' success to skill at office politics rather than to performance—whatever the truth of the matter. Some undoubtedly attribute their own lack of success to others' political power plays; some who have no interest in rising in the organization attribute others' rise to political maneuvering. This pattern of beliefs about rising in an organization because of politics as opposed to performance helps explain why so many executives are either laughed at or despised by people in the lower ranks—people of all generations, not just the young ones.

This difference in how people at different levels in organizations attribute success also helps explain what seems to be a generational difference but is primarily a difference based on organizational level.

Figure 5.4. Responses to the Statement, "In My Company, People Get Ahead Because of Their Skill at Office Politics," by Organizational Level.

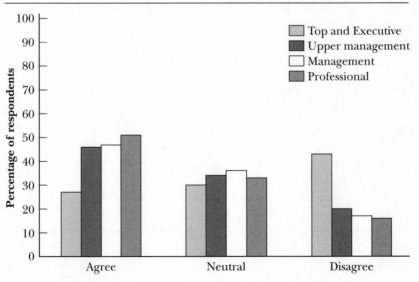

Older people are likely to be at higher levels than are younger people, so it appears as if older people are more skeptical of the politics explanation than are younger people. When we ran an analysis with both generation and organizational levels as factors, we found that organizational level explained almost all of the difference—that it didn't matter much what generation you were, what was most important was your level in your organization.

Organizational Politics Is a Problem— No Matter How Old (or Young) You Are

As we've discussed, people of different generations have the same fundamental attitudes toward office politics; the differences relate to the person's level in the organization, particularly when it comes to how employees think people get promoted. People high in an organization think they got there because of their performance; people lower in organizations are more likely to think that the people who are higher got there because of their skill at office politics.

It doesn't matter who is correct. In this case it truly is the perception that can cause a large-scale problem. If you think somebody got ahead because of her skill at office politics (read: kissing up) rather than because she's good at her job, what are you going to think about her? Worse, if she thinks she got ahead because she's confident, good at her job, and productive, but you think she got ahead because of office politics, are you really likely to trust her judgment on budgets or strategic planning or the markets? Quite possibly not. After all, if she's so confused about how she got ahead, how confused is she about other things?

Further, if you believe that the people in charge in your organization reward skill at office politics rather than good work and productivity, how much are you going to trust the organization? How much are you going to trust the people in upper management? How hard are you going to work to perform and do a good job?

Employees lower in organizations often think that people at higher levels are functionally incompetent. That the people higher in an organization don't see themselves as incompetent results in a disconnect between the people in the lower and higher levels in an organization.

How This Applies to You (Whether or Not You Are a Manager)

The reality is that political skills are important for success in organizations no matter your age. Organizations are run by people who have to interact with other people to get things done. Whether we like it or not, what that means is that others have to like us, trust us, and want to work with us if we are to get the work done and to be successful. (There are undoubtedly a few jobs where none of this matters, but we can't think of any offhand.) If you want to be successful in a job, it is better to be good at getting along with others (that is, good at political behavior) than it is to have people dislike you and avoid working with you.

Returning to the earlier example of Senior and Junior, management often chooses for political reasons to address these types of problems as "process" or "communication" issues within a group rather than as individual personnel issues. The result of this choice is an increase in cynicism and mistrust of management, and a stronger belief that decisions are driven by politics rather than by what is best for the business.

If you're a manager, we recommend that you be honest with your direct reports about the reality that office politics really does play a significant part in promotions. Employees may not like it, but the situation is unlikely to change as long as human beings are making promotion decisions, and at least you are giving them information they can act on. What employees can do is choose whether or not they want to learn how to be better at office politics.

If you're an employee with no direct reports, or someone (anyone!) who needs to manage up as well as manage down (and that is just about everyone in an organization), you similarly need to understand that politics is a part of work. You also need to realize that you can gain a great deal at work if you can successfully navigate through political waters that are more likely to be filled with sharks and piranhas than with guppies.

Being good at office politics is a skill that can be learned by anyone, though not everyone will be equally proficient. Just as some people are naturally good at math or tennis, others are naturally good at making people feel good, getting their ideas across, or being remembered by the people in power. But everyone can do some specific things that will help him or her become better at office politics.

If you aren't doing as well as you want to at managing office politics, you need to sit down and think hard about the difference between what you are doing and what others are doing who are more successful in the political sphere. Generally there are specific behaviors that people do that get them ahead in the office politics game. Are they having more lunches with people to find out what is going on in the organization? Are they spending more time walking around and less time doing their actual work? Are they taking on extra group or committee work so that different people can see them? When they're working on a team, are they perceived as being easy and fun to work with, as well as being good contributors?

You also might want to ask your manager for some coaching. A good manager can help you think through what you are or aren't doing to succeed politically within the organization. Once the thinking is done, it's helpful to create a list of action items that detail what you need to do and to learn.

For example, if you find you aren't doing a good job of networking with people outside your department, can you set up lunches with peers in other divisions? Are there internal committees you can ask to be on? If you aren't well known by people above you in the organization, can you have your boss take you to meetings so you can have more "face time"? Is there a mentoring program at your organization that you could ask to participate in?

For some people, the very thought of being "political" is distasteful. They think about the young, good-looking manager who does very little and seems to keep rising anyway—obviously because he knows who to suck up to. They remember the woman who recently got a promotion after having sat on an important committee— that did nothing productive but get her a lot of face time with the execs. They think of politics as demeaning and sort of sleazy. Though it may be distasteful, politics influences who gets what opportunities. That is the reality of organizational life. What you need to do is figure out what you can—and are willing—to do.

Of course, you may think through the whole issue and decide that you just can't be bothered—that it is beneath you, too much work for too little reward, too manipulative to stomach, or just morally repugnant. That's a fine decision to make, as long as you understand that you don't get to complain that others are getting ahead unfairly if you aren't even willing to get in the game! Remember, managing office politics effectively is a skill you can learn—and you don't have to lose your soul or self-respect while doing it. There are ways to be political at work without feeling unclean. After all, since when is it wrong, evil, or manipulative to have lunch with a peer when you're honestly interested in what he is doing?

Whatever degree of political proficiency someone achieves, people who don't rise in their organization may be suspicious of how those who did end up at the top levels got there. People higher in an organization need to understand that the political reality of working in an organization is that others are likely to be suspicious of how the higher-ups got to that level—and they aren't likely to presume the best. Helping others learn how *they* can use office politics to their advantage will go a long way toward helping them see your political skills in a more positive light.

What You Should Have Learned from This Chapter

- Different generations (by and large) have similar attitudes toward office politics, though they may express those attitudes slightly differently.
- People higher in organizations think they got there because of their hard work and strong performance.
- People lower in organizations think political behavior is more important for advancement than do people higher in organizations.
- Employees may not like it, but they generally understand that office politics is a reality. So if you're a manager, there's no need to pretend that office politics doesn't exist and has no real impact.
- You can improve at office politics by understanding the forces—views, perceptions, needs, preferences, stakes—that are shaping the political climate. What you want to do is learn how to manage the competing forces more effectively so that you can achieve what *you* want.

No One Really Likes Change

> People have a tough time with change.
> —Silent

Mergers, acquisitions, increased regulation, decreased regulation, downsizing, upsizing, rightsizing, RIFs, outsourcing, insourcing, reorganizing, restructuring, moving the deck chairs, upgrading the software, upgrading the hardware, changing the light bulbs, buying a new brand of toilet paper for the bathrooms—for better or worse, every organization is constantly changing. And people believe that the pace of change is getting more and more frenetic.

People have told us that one reason organizations like hiring younger people is that younger employees are more likely to embrace organizational change than are older employees. The stereotype is that older people dislike anything about their workplace being changed, and younger people love change. And not only younger people say this—we've heard it equally often from older people. As far as we can tell, people of all generations think that everyone else (other than themselves, of course) isn't as accepting of change as he or she should be.

What is it about changes within organizations that people of different generations complain about? Do people from different generations see each other as being open to change?

According to younger people, older people are convinced that change is a bad idea because

Things were better in the past. Anything that moves the organization away from where it was in the past, when it was the best it ever was, is a bad idea. Even if the organization is hemorrhaging money and will have to close shortly, it would be better for it to die than to change from the way it was in the past.

You shouldn't fix what isn't broken. Things seem to be working just fine, so why would you want to change it? It ain't broke, so don't fix it. (Or) You're trying to break it just so you have an excuse to fix it.

You don't understand the potential consequences of the change you are proposing. What about the unintended and unexpected consequences of a change? Sometimes there are good reasons for doing what we do the way we do it. Do you know what the domino effect of consequences will be if we change what we're doing?

They've seen it before. Often older employees have been around long enough that they've seen the same (or a similar) initiative attempted in the past. "There they go again," they say. Why, they wonder, do you expect it to work any better now than it did then?

According to older people, younger people want to change everything immediately. According to the stereotype, younger people are always saying,

If you just changed this . . . It may work well enough now, but it will work much better in the future if you change this and this and this! Just because the change I am suggesting didn't work in the past doesn't mean it isn't going to work now! Can't you see the potential?

Let's do something new! It's boring to do things the same way all the time, so why don't we change things around and shake things up a bit!

Maybe . . . Maybe if we make a few changes it will shake things loose and I'll get a chance to move up.

If you took these assumptions to their natural conclusion, you might think that you should introduce and go through organizational changes differently for older employees than you do for younger employees. But is this conclusion really correct? Are the assumptions accurate? Does one generation really like change more than another does? Do managers need to concoct different approaches to change for different age groups?

Research

The results we present here are based on responses to open-ended questions about retention, career challenges, and conflict with people of other generations. We didn't ask specific questions about change, so the results discussed in this chapter come from comments volunteered (unprompted) about change. What this means is that we don't know what the whole sample thinks about change; we know only what those who commented think about it. Having given that disclaimer, we add that discussions we have had with people about the results indicate that these results are consistent with what most people think when they move beyond generalizations and stereotypes.

Do older people actually resist change?
Do younger people actually embrace it?

The short answer to both questions is no. Older people don't have a knee-jerk reaction against change any more than younger people say "Right on, dude" every time a change is proposed.

In general, people from all generations are uncomfortable with change. Almost no one who participated in the study (only 12 people out of 2,500) said they actually liked change. Most said they were concerned, annoyed, scared, and agitated by change in the workplace.

> What you *can* face is working with people who have
> been in the organization for a long time and do not like to
> see changes in the workplace. This can be any age.
> —Silent

Older generations (Silents, Early Boomers, and Late Boomers) were significantly more likely than younger generations (Early Xers, Late Xers) to bring up change as an issue in their own careers, though they didn't necessarily say they were resistant to change.

Overall, respondents from all generations are typically not pleased about changes in their workplace. Although it is true that older people are concerned about change, they are not significantly more concerned than younger people are. Further, older people aren't concerned about change because it is different from what happened in the "good old days"; they're concerned about change for the same reasons younger people are. People of all generations are apprehensive that organizational changes

Will increase their workload

Will decrease their authority and power

Will decrease their resources (both budgetary and human)

People also often believe that changes are often

Unnecessary

Not communicated effectively

Disorganized

People of all generations are concerned about how organizational changes are going to affect *them*. Overall, the topics of respondents' comments fell into these five categories:

1. Doing the same work with fewer resources
2. Changes in both the internal and external environment
3. Technology changes
4. Change that is disorganized, unnecessary, or both
5. Resistance to change

Doing the Same Work with Fewer Resources. A key issue for all generations was "managing with less and trying to do as good of a job with less staff," as an Early Boomer said. All generations talked about how difficult it was to keep getting the work done with diminishing funding and resources. There were many comments that they sometimes felt as if management thought they should be able to do the same amount of work—or sometimes more!—with fewer people to do the job. Generally the feeling was that the idea that the same amount of work could be done at the same level of quality with fewer people was an example of management deluding themselves—or listening too closely to consultants who were validating management's delusions. People said that if the "strategic reduction" in staff also came with a similar "strategic reduction" in work, they wouldn't be concerned (unless they were the ones about to be laid off), but that wasn't what they said was happening. The suggestion was that management seemed to think that people and other resources could be eliminated without any effect on how much work would get done or what the quality of the work would be. Overall, there was great frustration with being asked to make changes that required more work when the resources for that work were being reduced or taken away altogether. Who can't identify with that?

Changes in the Internal and External Environment. Another concern that came up frequently with all generations was the "constantly changing work organization and environment," as an Early Boomer said. All generations talked about how quickly their organization's internal and external environments are changing and how much there is to keep up with. Structural changes to organizations happen often, and people talked about how they had to take time away from other things to understand how the structural change would (or often would not) directly affect how they got their work organized and done. Some discussed regulatory environments and the constant changes organizations have to keep up with to stay within the law. Others discussed the increase in globalization and the need to keep track of competitors, not just 12 or 1,200 miles away but even 12,000 miles away.

> *"Change" is scientific, "progress" is ethical; change is indubitable, whereas progress is a matter of controversy.*
> —BERTRAND RUSSELL (1872–1970), *Unpopular Essays*, 1950

Changes in Technology. People also talked about how the technology in the workplace was constantly changing and how those changes put an additional strain on their work. Although this problem was reported by people of all generations, it was mentioned far more frequently by older respondents. They pointed out that they hadn't grown up with computers as their younger colleagues had and that the constant small changes in technology were wearing. They said they understood why the changes were necessary and that they really tried to keep up, but that it just took a lot of time and was frustrating to them. Younger people didn't talk about this issue in the same way. Some mentioned that the constant technology changes were often as irritating as they were helpful. Others said they enjoyed keeping up on the newest and best options when it came to technological improvements in their work.

Disorganized and Unnecessary Changes. A fourth issue (shared by all generations) was how many changes seemed to be disorganized or unnecessary. For example, one Early Boomer said a career challenge was dealing with "multiple reorganizations at all levels . . . creating much confusion due to lack of integration of the various initiatives." Some respondents commented on the faddish nature of many changes. They suggested that it often seemed as though management made changes just for the sake of change—that the changes had no real functional reason, and were being made just because someone felt a need to change something. Respondents also suggested that management often seemed to make changes to obscure or take the focus off of problems that the company was having, rather than to fix the problems. They suggested that with more forethought and more proactive management, fewer changes would be necessary.

> Force without wisdom falls of its own weight.
> —Horace (Quintus Horatius Flaccus, 65–8 b.c.)

Resistance to Change. The fifth key issue had to do with others (of all generations) resisting or rejecting change. People in management especially commented on the difficulties they had with people who didn't want changes to happen and who had trouble dealing with the changes when they did happen. One respondent (a Silent) said that a primary management issue was "constant changes affecting personnel who do not adapt well to change." Managers said that in addition to having to deal with the changes themselves, they also had to help their employees—who didn't like and had trouble with the changes—deal with the changes. Some respondents talked about how people who had been in their organization for a long time seemed to spend a lot of time talking about the glory years and wanted to keep everything as it was then. There was also a lot of discussion about people who are threatened by changes and do everything they can to resist or sabotage the changes that are implemented. Just because people are told the change is going to happen doesn't mean they have to do anything to *help* it happen.

Is it true that people feel that generational conflict is in part a result of different attitudes toward change?

Even though people of all generations agreed that change is often a problem they don't want to deal with, perceptions about differences in attitudes toward change still cause conflict between the generations. When we asked people about generational conflict, we received 184 responses in which change was volunteered as an explanation for such conflict. The generations did not comment equally frequently about change being a point of conflict with people from other generations.

Contrary to the stereotypes, Silents did not say they had lots of conflict with younger people about change. In fact, they said that they had conflicts with older people, and people in general (not specifying a generation), more often than they did with younger people. Also contrary to the stereotype, Silents was the group most likely to say it liked change.

Early Boomers also said they have conflicts with older people (including people of their own generation) about changes in the workplace. They said they think older people have problems with change and that they have conflicts about change with older people more often than with younger people. (They have conflicts with younger people about different things, such as decorum at work.) It is interesting that the respondents from this generation complained about others' resistance to change, but none of them said they liked change themselves.

Late Boomers and Early Xers commented more frequently than the other generations about other people having problems dealing with change. As expected, they commented frequently about older people having problems with change. They also commented frequently about conflicts with people in general (not specifying a generation) regarding change.

The people who most often said they liked change were the Silents and the Early Xers. Whereas many people would expect the Early Xers to say they liked change, few would expect Silents to say it more frequently than any other generation.

However, when you think about the Silents' life stage, their response to change makes perfect sense: Silents are currently thinking actively about retirement and may be more likely than other groups to embrace change and like the potential changes, rather than resist them. The change that is likely to come is one that many Silents have been looking forward to for many years—in direct contrast to the less pleasant organizational changes that many of the other generations are anticipating.

In fact, what we see is that older people are at least as likely as younger people to blame older people for causing conflict about change. Younger people are likely to focus equally on people in general and on older people in particular. Very few people focus on younger people as being a source of conflict about change, though the responses of the younger people show that they are not more gung-ho about change than older people are. It's more accurate to say that older people are blamed for conflict about change, though they don't necessarily dislike it more than anybody else does.

So if older and younger people dislike change equally, who *does* like change? Is it a matter of level in the organization?

Do people high in organizations like organizational change more than people lower in the organization?

In general, people from all organizational levels are uptight about change and see dealing effectively with change as an important challenge they face in their careers.

People in management positions say more often than people at any other level that change is a career challenge for them. When they say this they're talking about change in general—not specific kinds of change. This makes sense, as they have to deal with all different kinds of change in their jobs as managers. They are not at the strategic level (top or executive level), designing a new organizational structure and handing it off to someone else to make it work. They are at the implementation level, having to take the organizational changes that are handed to them and make them work—somehow. And though they say they do see some resistance to change, they don't say it comes from older people.

People in upper management, in the executive ranks, and in C-level positions (such as CIO, CFO, CEO) also say that organizational change is a critical career challenge for them. They are the ones who generally have to think through the direction of the organization and what strategic changes are necessary. They talk about resistance a bit less often than middle managers do, though they do say they encounter it.

People in the professional ranks talk about dealing with change less often than do managers at the different levels.

It is clear from the responses that people at the management level and above see dealing effectively with change as a critical career issue for them. They write often about resistance to change as a recurrent problem that is frustrating for them. It isn't clear that executives and managers like organizational change more than anyone else does, but they do say that it is a career challenge far more often than other people do. Interestingly, executives and managers do not comment about change being a point of conflict between generations more often than people at other levels do. They talk about resistance to change, but don't blame it for generational conflict. They think that resistance to change is endemic to all generations!

Almost No One Really Likes Change

Resistance to change is typically not about older people wanting to turn the clock back to a "kinder, gentler" time that probably never existed except on TV. Yes, older people may comment more about change being a problem than younger people do. And yes, both older and younger people say that older people have more of a problem with change than younger people do. But the content of the comments is generally the same—people of all generations

- Do not see change as a positive thing
- Do not like change because it is likely to reduce their resources
- Do not like change because it is seen as unnecessary and isn't communicated effectively
- Do not embrace change because they think it probably will not be implemented well

Resistance to organizational change is not fundamentally about age or generation, but rather about what the change is and how it is going to be implemented.

Top-level managers see change as an opportunity to strengthen the business by aligning operations with strategy, to take on new professional challenges and risks, and to advance their careers. For many employees, however, including middle managers, change is neither sought after nor welcomed. It is disruptive and intrusive. It upsets the balance. . . . [Managers at all levels] must put themselves in their employees' shoes to understand how change looks from that perspective and to examine the terms of the "personal compacts" between employees and the company [Strebel, 1996, pp. 86–87].

Often when companies make changes, their top-level managers talk about the employees being fundamentally resistant to change. Our research shows that people have rational reasons for resisting change. Given the generally negative attitude managers and executives can expect to encounter with regard to the change, what do the literature and our research suggest that people should do?

How This Applies to You

As an employee being affected by proposed changes, if you are unhappy or concerned about them, why not ask for further explanations? As an employee, you owe it to yourself to understand the changes you are being told to enact. The more you understand the purpose and potential benefits of the changes, the more likely you are to be able to help the change succeed.

Another positive outcome of asking for more information about the change is that it signals to the people who designed the change that (1) you are interested in what is happening and have good intentions, and (2) you don't have all the information you need to help *them* succeed. Your asking for more information for this reason may cause them to substantially increase communication about the change, and you can find out what you need to know.

If You Are a Manager

Some people just don't like change. For them it is a personal issue, because they intuitively frame change in terms of potential loss rather than in terms of keeping the status quo or potential gains. For example:

Tim (the boss) has told David (the direct report) about a change to his job. David is really upset about the change, and Tim keeps telling him (over and over again), "David, you're just going to have to learn to deal with change. It isn't that big an issue. Just deal with it." Tim's response does nothing to make David feel better about the change; rather, it makes David feel as if Tim has no understanding of what David does. And if Tim has no understanding of what David does, how can David possibly believe Tim when he says that the change won't have an effect on David's work?

Tim mentioned David's (to him, disproportionate) response to Andrea, a manager in another division who was also going to be affected by the change. Tim wanted to know what, if anything, he could do to help David deal with the change. Andrea pointed out to Tim that the core of David's work (about 80%) wasn't going to change at all. Which building he walked to was likely to change, but what he actually *did* wasn't going to change. Further, the 20% that was going to change was actually going to make David's life easier and eliminate some work that he had been complaining about having to do in the first place. Andrea suggested that if Tim framed the change in that way and pointed out those specifics to David, David might be less upset by and resistant to the change that was going to happen.

Tim thought Andrea's idea was great (making a note that he should frame things that way in the future), and he went to talk with David. After he explained the change to David using Andrea's framing, David was much less concerned. He wasn't entirely happy (because he really doesn't like change), but he understood what was going to happen. David understood that the real, functional change wasn't terribly large, and that in the end the change was going to benefit him.

In this case, just reframing or recasting the change helped a great deal to reduce anxiety and overcome resistance to the change, despite David's personal aversion to it.

You notice that we haven't mentioned anyone's generation in this example; all the people happened to be from the same generation— they were all Early Xers. As Andrea pointed out in another conversation, resistance to change has nothing to do with age; it is all about the willingness and ability to deal with ambiguity and about how much you have to gain or lose with the change. Some people are just better at managing the tension that comes with ambiguity and at becoming proactive when faced with a potential loss. Like an aptitude for math or the piano, the aptitude for dealing with change varies among people, but everyone can increase his or her level of skill.

In a different example, a call center was going to be closed, and all the employees were (understandably) very upset and unsure about what was going to happen to them. Some of them reacted by shutting down and fretting about the future while failing to do anything proactive to assure themselves of a position. Others fretted, but also decided that doing something proactive would make them feel better about the situation, so they spent time looking through other open positions within the organization and applying for them. Some even went to their supervisors and asked for immediate training to make them appropriate candidates for open positions. Some of the people in the call center were just better at dealing with the ambiguity and putting together a plan for what to do next. They weren't less concerned, upset, or angry about the change; they were just better at handling it. As a manager, there are specific things you can do (like Andrea suggested and Tim did) to help people deal with the constant changes that are inevitable in organizations. Our best advice is "Explain, explain, explain." And "Don't set your expectations too high."

Whatever the general attitude toward change, managers and executives need to communicate about any specific change: what it is, why it is happening, who it is going to affect, and what its consequences will be. Sometimes executives think it is better not to share the information—even with their managers—because people may react negatively to it. The question you need to ask yourself is whether the truth is more positive and less scary than the rumors that are going around—and if the truth is more scary, should you even be making the changes? The people you're talking to aren't your children—whatever their age. They are adults you have hired to do a job, not children you're trying to protect (which is patronizing anyway).

> Management has to do a good job at selling change.
> —Late Boomer

You need to be especially careful about how you articulate the change, because our research shows that there is a strong relationship between age and organizational level and how well upper management is perceived to be communicating. Early Xers and people lower in organizations are typically more critical of upper management's communication than are older employees and employees who are higher in organizations. Therefore it is especially important to communicate well (and thoroughly) if you want to bring Early Xers and people lower in the organization on board with the change.

Employees of all ages need to be told as clearly as possible what the change is and what effect it is expected to have. Many change initiatives are perceived by employees as having no real impact on how the organization functions; changes are made, but the people doing the actual work don't really see that anything has altered. The executives might think there was a fundamental shift or realignment, but people much lower down the ladder think that the only shift was in the minds of the executives!

You may understand the reasons for the change and have a belief about its real impact because you've been in meetings about it and have had time to think through it, but many of your people (whatever their generation) have not been in those meetings and therefore don't have the background or understanding of the change that you have. Older people may want to know how the changes are better than the old system; younger people want to know how the changes will help in the future. Whatever the change is, you need to provide an adequate justification for why the change is going to happen. And we mean *adequate justification*—which does not include *because we think it's a good idea and we said so* (in whatever more polite terms). Many people need to understand why something is happening; some just need to understand that you thought it through. Either way, they need to hear the justification. And *everybody* wants to know how he or she will be affected.

We have no evidence that says you need to alter how you communicate about the change to fit generational attitudes toward change. A better strategy is to focus more on what type of person you are talking to about the change than on how old he or she is. Different types of people need different types of information to understand what is happening around them. For example, people who are more detail oriented (like engineers) are going to be interested in the details of the change. People who are more inter-

"If we can just get beyond this 'I'm the boss' mentality and concentrate on a simple 'What I say goes' outlook, I think this will all work out."

ested in vision and mission statements are likely to care less about the details and more about how the change is going to have a positive impact on the mission of the organization. Some people are focused on the bottom-line financials more than anything else, and they're going to be more interested in how the change is going to affect that. Finally, some people are more focused on how the employees are going to react and are going to be more interested in information about any cultural effect the change is going to cause and how to deal with it.

It is critical that executives set up systems that support and reinforce the change. Many change initiatives fail because no one has bothered to realign the functional structure of the organization to reflect the change. People are more likely to think a change has teeth and get on board with it if the change is reinforced by the organization's structure and processes.

Executives often say that people in their organization need to trust that the change is a good idea, that it will work out and be for the best—even with no explanation. Would you? (If you would, we have a piece of prime real estate you might be interested in.) There have been too many examples of people not knowing what they're doing (or knowing and doing bad things anyway—think Enron), and there's too much at stake just to trust blindly. (What's more, as we discussed in the chapter on trust, part of building trust in an organization is about how managers explain their actions and the company's decisions.) Although overall trust may not be high, you can probably count on a bit more trust from people who are older and higher in the organization than you can from people who are younger and lower in the organization.

But you shouldn't count on trust; you need to be able to sell the change on its merits. Why is the change going to make the company better? What is it going to do to make employees' work better, easier, or more productive? How is it going to lead to higher pay, more time off, or more and better opportunities? If you can answer these questions about the change, you'll probably be able to convince both older and younger people that it is a good idea, whether they trust the organization or not!

Many people believe it is better not to provide such information to the people below them. They believe that providing information causes more questioning—which people who can't justify what they're doing always perceive as being a bad thing. (It seems to us that if you can't justify what you're doing, you shouldn't be doing it in the first place—sort of like the old rule that you shouldn't do anything you wouldn't want published on the front page of your hometown newspaper.) At minimum, it is bad management practice not to explain what is happening and why it is happening. Worse, your employees might perceive your inadequate explanations as an insult to them as working professionals. It says very uncomplimentary things about how good you are at your job (as the manager or executive) if you feel that the only way you can get your employees to do what you want them to do is by hiding information from them, manipulating them, or lying to them. We understand that many executives believe that this is how they should manage; we also know that this approach does nothing but decrease the trust between professional employees and the executives they report to. (For more discussion of these ideas, please refer to Principle 3.)

People like changes that they think will make things better for them personally, and they dislike (dread, in fact) changes that they think will make things worse. As the old saying goes, better the devil you know than the one you don't; people usually assume that any change is most likely going to be for the worse. What top-level managers need to figure out is how the change is going to make things better for the employees and then communicate that effectively.

There are many similarities in how to communicate effectively with people from different generations about organizational change. As we've discussed, employees of all generations have the same general concerns about changes: that changes are going to have a negative impact on them, that the changes won't be communicated or implemented well, and that there isn't a good reason for the proposed changes. Fundamentally, resisting change is about being threatened by it and not about chronological age or the generation the employee was born into. So don't say that older people are resisting the change or that younger people are all for it. Neither statement is true, and both will cause you problems.

In an earlier era, employees could easily be made to "buy into" change through coercion. As the old bad-manager joke goes, "Everybody who is in favor of my plan, signify by saying 'Aye.' All opposed, signify by saying 'I resign.'"

But in the modern world, employees are very familiar with—and often excellent practitioners of—the techniques of passive resistance, patience, and sabotage when they don't buy into proposed changes. As we've all seen, all that employees need to do is to do nothing, and eventually the "change" is likely to go away. So it becomes vital for leaders to overcome, or at least mitigate, resistance to changes that are essential to their organization's prosperity or even its survival.

Both older and younger people say older people are more resistant to change than younger people are, but is that because they are older or because they think they are going to lose as a result of the change? Our research shows that resistance to change among employees relates more to their feeling threatened with the potential loss of authority, power, or resources than it does to their age or generation. If a change is going to cause losses in the short

*"No, Hoskins, you're not going to do it just
because I'm telling you to do it. You're going to
do it because you believe in it."*

run (and many of them do), then you have to expect (and accept)
resistance and make the case for why the change is going to make
people's work lives better in the long run. Your chances of success
are greatly increased if you can effectively communicate that the
change is needed, that the change will be implemented effectively,
and that the people affected by the change will be treated fairly.

What You Should Have Learned from This Chapter

- Both older and younger people believe (erroneously) that
  older people dislike change more than younger people do.
- People of all generations dislike change because they think it
  is likely to affect them negatively (for example, because
  they're going to lose power or resources).
- People of all generations think changes are often instituted or
  communicated poorly.

- Older people resist change because they've seen it implemented poorly in the past, and they have no evidence that it's going to be handled any better this time—but, on the whole, they don't resist change more than younger people.
- Some people do have more problems with change than others do—but that isn't because of their age; it is because they're more fearful of loss than they are hopeful of gain.
- Managers and executives don't like change much more than do people lower in organizations.
- If you're instituting a change, you can't just expect people to trust you and go along with the change happily—or even quietly.
- To increase the likelihood of success in a change effort, leaders must explain why the change is necessary, explain what actual effect the change is going to have, and set up organizational systems that reinforce the change.

Loyalty Depends on the Context, Not on the Generation

Have you ever heard anyone say that younger people are intrinsically disloyal to their employers? We have—and not just during this research project. We've heard complaints that young people aren't loyal to their organizations, as demonstrated (people say) by the fact that they job-hop, they don't feel appropriate levels of gratitude to their employer, they feel a sense of entitlement, they don't work the same long hours their older peers do, and so on.

To be more specific, what people say (both younger and older people) is that young people are no longer loyal to their organizations *in the way that young people (now older) were in the past.* They say that young people's loyalty to self, profession, area, family, hobbies, friends, boss, coworkers, pets, and just about anything else you can think of is greater than their loyalty to their organizations. People complain about the supposed lack of loyalty as if it were a defect in the upbringing of the young people—as if they haven't been taught to appreciate what they've got.

> I'm just ahead of the boomer generation (I was born in
> 1939). Throughout my career I've felt pressure from this
> generation in terms of "Get out of the way so I can advance,
> you old person." My generation believes in loyalty and putting
> others first. Many boomers are "just for themselves."
> —Silent

But what do people mean when they say "loyalty"? What is loyalty at work? Is it that every individual employee should put the organization's needs ahead of his or her own? Should people just sit down and shut up and do what they're told? Should people stay with an organization that is underpaying them or treating them poorly? Should they not look for other opportunities when they don't feel that they are being given adequate opportunities by their organization? What exactly does it mean when someone says that people aren't loyal to their organization anymore? Is there a disconnect between the different generations' definitions of loyalty?

We'll start by considering the dictionary definitions of loyalty:

Dedication—complete and wholehearted faithfulness

Feelings of allegiance or duty to someone or something (such as an organization)

The act of binding yourself (intellectually or emotionally) to a course of action

The quality or state of being loyal (having unswerving allegiance; being faithful to a cause, ideal, or custom)

Putting that definition into a work context and thinking about your own situation, would you say that it describes your level of commitment to your employer? Would you say that those feelings would prevent you from accepting a better offer with a different organization? Would they cause you to stay in your job even if you thought you were being treated badly? Do you consistently put the organization's needs ahead of the needs of your family? Is it really reasonable to call someone disloyal if he or she accepts a better position elsewhere? Is it reasonable to expect people to put their loyalty to their current employer ahead of their loyalty to their family? And do people today even want to stay with their organizations for the rest of their working lives?

As we began to consider loyalty as a subject for our research, we started to pay close attention to all mentions of the word. Amid all the talk about loyalty, two questions came up in conversation more than others.

1. How long do people think others should stay with an organization?
2. How hard (how many hours) do people work for their organization?

Using these two themes, we developed a number of questions to focus our research in this area. Our goal was to answer the question of supposed differences in loyalty more concretely and, ultimately, to help organizations create an atmosphere in which people want to be loyal (as in "work hard" and "stay a long time").

With regard to what people think about how long people should stay with an organization, we developed the following questions:

Are the generations different in whether they want to stay with their organization for the rest of their career?

Are the generations different in how long they think people *should* stay with their organization?

Are the generations different in terms of whether respondents themselves are going to stay with their organization?

Do younger generations change jobs more frequently than older generations did at the same age?

With regard to the question of how hard people work for their organization, we asked concrete questions:

Are the generations different in terms of how many hours they work in a week?

Are the generations different in terms of how frequently they work on weekends?

Research

We asked people whether they want to stay with their organization, how long they think people should stay with an organization, how many jobs they've had (and over what time period in their lives), how many hours they work per week, and how many weekends they work per month.

Are the generations different in terms of wanting to stay with their organization for the rest of their career?

We asked people to respond to the statement, "I would like to stay with this organization for the rest of my working life." What we found is that people from every generation said they would like to stay with their organization; the older they were, the more likely they were to say that (see Figure 7.1). Similarly, people higher in the organization said that more than people lower in the organization (Figure 7.2).

Are the generations different in terms of how long they think people should stay with their organization?

We often hear people say that one of the biggest differences between the generations is that they have different beliefs about what are the minimum and maximum lengths of time that an employee should stay with an organization. We have heard people say that younger people are more likely to think that there is no minimum amount of time they should spend at a job (they can leave after three months if they don't like it, and it won't matter), while also believing that there is a maximum amount of time they should spend with any organization (you shouldn't stay more than five years or you'll get stale). We have also heard people say that, con-

Figure 7.1. Percentage of Respondents Agreeing with the Statement, "Yes, I Would Like to Stay with This Organization for the Rest of My Working Life," by Generation.

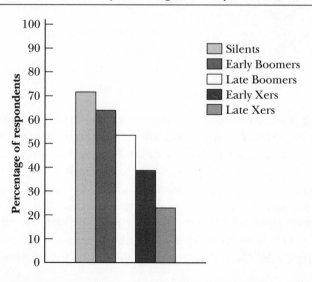

Figure 7.2. Percentage of Respondents Agreeing with the Statement, "Yes, I Would Like to Stay with This Organization for the Rest of My Working Life," by Organizational Level.

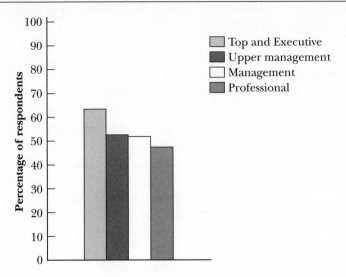

versely, older generations think there is a minimum amount of time to be spent with any one organization to show that you're not flaky (at least a couple of years, preferably more), but that the longer you spend with an organization, the better you look to other potential employers.

So we asked people these questions: "What is the minimum amount of time people should spend with an organization?" and "What is the maximum amount of time people should spend with an organization?"

Minimum Time. What the respondents told us is very different from what we hear people saying. The most frequent response from people of all generations is that there is no minimum amount of time that it is appropriate to stay with an organization (see Table 7.1). Contrary to conventional wisdom, it was the Early Xers who were the most likely to say that one to two years was the minimum amount of time to spend with an organization. Silents, Early Boomers, and Late Xers were more likely to say that there was no minimum time. Therefore the data show that the minimum time

Table 7.1. Responses to the Question, "What Is the Minimum Time a Person Should Stay at an Organization?" by Generation.

	Silents	Early Boomers	Late Boomers	Early Xers	Late Xers	Overall
No minimum	43%	41%	33%	31%	39%	36%
Less than a year	0%	1%	1%	1%	3%	1%
1–2 years	23%	26%	28%	38%	37%	31%
3–4 years	21%	19%	24%	22%	13%	21%
5–6 years	8%	9%	12%	7%	6%	9%
7–8 years	0%	0%	1%	0%	0%	0%
9–10 years	2%	1%	0%	0%	1%	1%
More than 10 years	3%	3%	2%	1%	0%	2%

people think others should stay with an organization is not the result of a generational difference. The real difference shows up when we look at responses in terms of employees' level in the organization (see Table 7.2).

When we ran the same analysis by level in the organization, a couple of interesting results appeared. The most frequent response from all levels was that there is no minimum amount of time an individual should stay with an organization. Beyond that, professionals were more likely than other groups to say that there was no minimum required, or at most the minimum was one to two years, whereas people in the top and executive levels said that the minimum amount of time people should spend in an organization is three to four years.

Maximum Time. Overall, 83% of respondents said there was no maximum amount of time people should spend with an organization. (See Table 7.3 for responses sorted by generation.) Consistent with the stereotype, Gen Xers were more likely than any other group to say that the maximum amount of time an employee should stay with an organization is somewhere between five and eight years. With the Gen Xers there is a fear of being in a job or

124   RETIRING THE GENERATION GAP

Table 7.2. Responses to the Question, "What Is the Minimum Time a Person Should Stay at an Organization?" by Organizational Level.

	Top and Executive	Upper Management	Management	Professional
No minimum	32%	31%	33%	39%
Less than a year	0%	2%	0%	2%
1–2 years	26%	30%	29%	35%
3–4 years	29%	24%	23%	17%
5–6 years	10%	10%	11%	5%
7–8 years	0%	0%	0%	0%
9–10 years	0%	1%	1%	1%
More than 10 years	2%	1%	2%	1%

organization for so long that they are trapped and don't have any other options if they need to leave. It has been suggested that the fear has its origins in this generation's childhood experience of witnessing the mass layoffs of the 1970s and 1980s. During that time, many Gen Xers saw their parents (or their friends' parents) being laid off from long-term professional positions and having no options in part because they had been with one employer for so long. Now adults themselves, they have the idea that if they change organizations periodically, they will be less likely to become trapped. Another explanation is that they think they're going to go stale if they've been in one place for too long. (Incidentally, both of these issues can be virtually eliminated with good developmental planning—see Principle 9 for more information on this topic.)

There were no differences by level in the organization (see Table 7.4) or by generation. The most common response from respondents of all generations was that there was no maximum amount of time an individual should spend with an organization.

What do these results say about loyalty? What it means is that one generation isn't more (or less) loyal than another when it comes to beliefs about how long people should stay with an organization.

Table 7.3. Responses to the Question, "What Is the Maximum Time a Person Should Stay at an Organization?" by Generation.

	Silents	Early Boomers	Late Boomers	Early Xers	Late Xers	Overall
No maximum	85%	86%	85%	78%	75%	83%
Less than a year	0%	0%	0%	0%	2%	0%
1–2 years	0%	0%	0%	0%	1%	0%
3–4 years	1%	1%	1%	2%	3%	2%
5–6 years	2%	2%	2%	5%	5%	3%
7–8 years	3%	3%	2%	5%	3%	3%
9–10 years	5%	4%	5%	6%	4%	5%
More than 10 years	3%	3%	4%	4%	7%	4%

Table 7.4. Responses to the Question, "What Is the Maximum Time a Person Should Stay at an Organization?" by Organizational Level.

	Top and Executive	Upper Management	Management	Professional
No maximum	81%	83%	83%	83%
Less than a year	0%	0%	0%	0%
1–2 years	0%	0%	0%	0%
3–4 years	2%	1%	2%	2%
5–6 years	4%	3%	3%	4%
7–8 years	4%	4%	3%	3%
9–10 years	8%	5%	5%	5%
More than 10 years	3%	3%	5%	3%

*Are the generations different in terms of whether respondents
themselves are going to stay with their organization?*

Another question related to the issue of loyalty is whether or not
people think they will be with their organization in three years.
They could respond Yes, No, or Not sure. (Results are illustrated
in Figures 7.3 and 7.4.)

The results are much as we would expect. What we found is
that Silents say no at a higher rate than other older generations;
they're planning to retire and move on to another type of work or
simply retire. Some say they would think less about retirement if
there were more for them in their current job, but that they intend
to retire if things stay the same. (For a discussion of what people
from this generation say might make them want to stick around,
see the chapter on retention, Principle 8.)

Early and Late Boomers say yes, they do see themselves being
with their organization in three years. More than two-thirds of the
people from the Early and Late Xer groups said they weren't going
to be with their organization in three years or that they weren't

**Figure 7.3. Responses to the Question, "Do You See Yourself
Being with Your Organization in Three Years?" by Generation.**

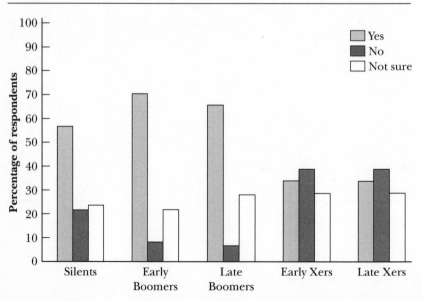

sure if they would be. So Early Boomers and Late Boomers are significantly more likely than are Gen Xers to say they'll be with their organizations in three years.

Unlike some other issues, what level you are in an organization has less of an effect than what generation you are from (what age you are) on whether you say you are going to stay with your organization. So what we see here fits the conventional wisdom: people from older generations (Early and Late Boomers) are more likely than people from younger generations (Early and Late Xers) to say they intend to stay with the organization. Some people would say that this means older generations are more loyal to their organization than are younger generations. Others would counter that, saying Silents are more disloyal because they are the most likely to leave.

But perhaps there is an explanation for the behavior of the younger generations beyond crass disloyalty or opportunism. First of all, occasionally life intervenes and alters what a person had

Figure 7.4. Responses to the Question, "Do You See Yourself Being with Your Organization in Three Years?" by Organizational Level.

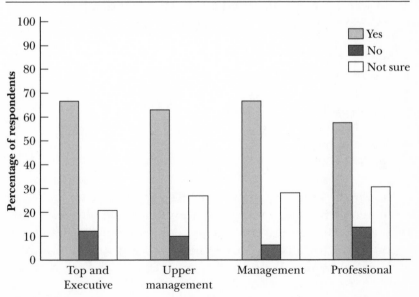

planned to do. There are any number of life factors external to the job itself that could cause someone—especially someone earlier in her career—to have to change organizations, whatever her preference.

Second, job engagement—how much someone actually likes her work—plays a critical role in her staying in her job. Earlier in a person's career (typically, when she is younger), she has less experience and is less sure of what she likes and what her options are, so she is more likely to think about moving to a different job that is more aligned with what she thinks she will want. As time goes on, she gets a better idea of what she enjoys, and the jobs she searches out are closer to what she enjoys, so she stays in them longer. So perhaps the movement in the earlier years of an individual's career is more about learning and less about opportunism than people might think.

With these ideas in mind, we asked people how frequently they had actually changed jobs during specific time periods in their lives. We wanted to see whether people from older generations actually reported changing jobs less frequently than did people from younger generations.

Do younger generations change jobs more frequently than older generations did at the same age?

To answer that question, we asked people how many jobs they had held during specific time periods in their lives:

- Age 20 to 25
- Age 26 to 30
- Age 31 to 35
- Age 36 to 40
- Age 41 to 45
- Age 46 to 50
- Age 51 to 55

Using the information provided by respondents, we looked to see if people from different generations had held different numbers of jobs during the same time periods in their lives. (Results are reported in Appendix F.) What we found was very straightforward—and very interesting. Between the ages of 20 and 25, Early Xers did hold more jobs than the Silents and Early and Late Boomers did at that time in their lives, and they held more jobs than the Late Xers are currently reporting. Why is this? Is it just that Early Xers were more flighty at that age than people were before and have been since (which is the common explanation)? Probably not—so what is a more reasonable explanation?

> The ease with which they move from job to job—doesn't appear
> to be any loyalty to the organization that trains you, etc.
> —Early Boomer

When you look at changes in norms over the past 50 years, what you find is that until Gen X, it wasn't as common for college students to have real jobs during the school year. On average, the Silents and the Early Boomers were much less likely to have such jobs during college than were later generations (and than people do now). What that means is that people from Gen X would be more likely to have had several jobs during college—typically the ages between 18 and 23. In other words, it isn't that Early and Late Xers have held six jobs in the three years between college graduation and when they turned 25; they were just much more likely to have had jobs while they were in college. Some people suggest this makes these employees more valuable to organizations because they will come out of college with real job experience in addition to an education.

There aren't any statistically significant differences among generations in the number of jobs held between the ages of 26 and 30. During this period, Early Xers do change jobs more frequently than did Late Boomers and Silents. However, the Early Xers' rate of job change is roughly equivalent to what was reported by Early Boomers, indicating that this is not a generational trend.

Between the ages of 31 and 35, the pattern switches. Although Silents and Early Boomers do report that they changed jobs slightly more frequently than did Late Boomers and Early Xers, the differences among the generations in how frequently they change jobs is too small to be meaningful.

Between the ages of 36 and 40, what you see is that older generations actually changed jobs more frequently than people from younger generations did. Silents and Early Boomers changed jobs more frequently than did Late Boomers. The number for Early Xers is probably artificially low, as when they responded to the survey they had not yet left the 36–40 age range.

After the age of 41, there is no significant difference in frequency of job change by generation. It doesn't matter what generation respondents were from; they were very unlikely to change jobs at all. After the age of 41, people reported that they changed jobs not more than once every 10 years on average.

What does this all mean? It means that younger people don't change jobs more frequently than older people did at the same age. So the next time you're tempted to say that younger people change jobs more frequently and therefore are more disloyal, resist the temptation.

What the few differences among the generations suggest is that the rate of job change probably has more to do with the economy than it does with the temperament and loyalty (or lack thereof) of any particular generation. If the economy is good, people are more likely to move because better opportunities are available. If the economy is bad, people are less likely to move voluntarily. So from an employer's perspective, there is both an upside and a downside to a good economy. When you have a good economy, you make more money, but you also have more trouble holding on to the best workers.

We've seen that when it comes to job hopping, younger people are no less loyal to their organizations than older people are. Now if you want to say they're less loyal to the organization because they don't work as hard as older people do, that's a different subject.

Are the generations different in how many hours they work in a week?

Our question, "How many hours do you work in a typical week?" received 3,200 responses. Table 7.5 shows the responses sorted by generation; in Table 7.6, responses are sorted by organizational level.

There is no short answer to the question of whether older people work more hours than younger people do, because the data are complicated. People at higher levels in an organization work more hours than do people at lower levels. Thus, on average, people who

Table 7.5. Responses to the Question, "How Many Hours Do You Work in a Typical Week?" by Generation.

	Silents	Early Boomers	Late Boomers	Early Xers	Late Xers	Overall
20 or fewer	6%	2%	2%	3%	34%	4%
21–25 hours	2%	1%	0%	1%	10%	1%
26–30 hours	1%	1%	1%	1%	7%	1%
31–35 hours	3%	2%	1%	1%	7%	2%
36–40 hours	21%	19%	13%	21%	16%	18%
41–45 hours	27%	28%	23%	25%	11%	25%
46–50 hours	16%	20%	27%	21%	8%	21%
51–55 hours	12%	11%	14%	13%	3%	12%
56–60 hours	7%	10%	10%	9%	3%	9%
61–65 hours	3%	5%	5%	2%	0%	4%
66–70 hours	1%	1%	2%	2%	0%	2%
71–75 hours	0%	0%	1%	0%	1%	0%
76–80 hours	1%	0%	0%	0%	0%	0%
More than 81 hours	0%	0%	0%	0%	1%	0%

are executives work more hours than people who are managers, who in turn work more hours than people who are professionals. Because older people are found more often at higher levels than are younger people, it sometimes appears that older people work more hours.

> Younger folks get angry and defiant at the thought of working overtime. Older generation sees this as a disloyalty.
> —Late Boomer

Within the top and executive ranks there is no generational difference in how many hours people work. These individuals just work a lot of hours—more than anyone else in the organization— regardless of their age. In upper management and management

**Table 7.6. Responses to the Question,
"How Many Hours Do You Work in a
Typical Week?" by Organizational Level.**

	Top and Executive	Upper Management	Management	Professional
20 or fewer	0%	0%	0%	3%
21–25 hours	0%	0%	0%	1%
26–30 hours	0%	0%	0%	2%
31–35 hours	0%	0%	2%	3%
36–40 hours	2%	9%	12%	34%
41–45 hours	11%	20%	32%	32%
46–50 hours	27%	29%	27%	15%
51–55 hours	19%	19%	14%	6%
56–60 hours	22%	12%	9%	3%
61–65 hours	9%	7%	3%	1%
66–70 hours	6%	2%	1%	0%
71–75 hours	1%	1%	0%	0%
76–80 hours	1%	1%	0%	0%
More than 81 hours	0%	0%	0%	0%

positions, Late Boomers and Early Xers reported working more hours than did Silents and Early Boomers. This makes sense because the longer you have been in management, the more you have learned (one hopes) and the more efficient you have become at managing and leading. In other words, the more you have learned from your experiences, the more you know what you need and don't need to do.

This pattern is true only in the management ranks; professional and first-level people of all generations on average work about the same number of hours. So although it is true that younger people overall work fewer hours than older people do, within a given management position, younger people on average work more hours than older people do.

Warning! Statistics!

If we were you and had read the preceding section (without being the ones who conducted the research), we would be trying to figure out why the results were wrong—because they were so contrary to what we expected. One possible explanation is something called a *response bias:* among members of certain demographic groups (such as men and women), researchers find that there is a systematic (and measurable) difference in how people respond to certain types of questions. So what about in this case? Is there any evidence that younger people systematically overestimate how much they work or that older people systematically underestimate how much they work? No, there is no evidence that older (or younger) people do this. Just in case there is some sort of response bias, we searched the responses to other items for a pattern that would indicate that different generations respond fundamentally differently (for example, Early Boomers consistently respond with 3 when Late Xers respond with 5). We didn't find any of this type of systematic difference either. Because there is no evidence of a systematic bias, we assume that people of all generations are about equally truthful.

Are the generations different in how frequently they work on weekends?
We asked people how many weekends they worked per month. As shown in Table 7.7, results indicate that there are no statistically significant differences among the generations in how many weekends per month people work.

But what about organizational level? Do people who are higher in organizations work more weekends than people who are lower in organizations? Yes, they do. As shown in Table 7.8, people in the top and executive ranks report working more weekends than do people at other levels in organizations. Professionals are least likely to say that they work on weekends.

**Table 7.7. Responses to the Question,
"How Frequently Do You Work on
Weekends?" by Generation.**

	Silents	Early Boomers	Late Boomers	Early Xers	Late Xers	Overall
One weekend per month	26%	28%	35%	34%	15%	31%
Two weekends per month	21%	25%	23%	22%	16%	23%
Three weekends per month	8%	9%	8%	8%	8%	8%
Every weekend	18%	11%	9%	7%	25%	11%
I do not work weekends	28%	27%	26%	29%	36%	28%

So within a level in an organization, do younger people work fewer weekends? No, they don't. Gen X managers are just as likely to work one weekend a month as are Silent managers, and Early Boomer professionals are not more likely than Gen X professionals to work on weekends.

Loyalty Depends on the Context, Not on the Generation

What these results show is that younger generations aren't appreciably less loyal than older generations. So why do people think that younger generations are less loyal? What has happened? And do organizations really need to focus on loyalty issues with younger people more than with anyone else?

One explanation for why people say that younger generations are less loyal is that there has been a significant change in the implicit work contract between employers and employees. In the good old days, people were much more loyal to their organizations—and the organizations were much more loyal to them. Specifically, people stayed with organizations for their entire work life because the implicit contract was that if they stayed loyal to the organization

**Table 7.8. Responses to the Question,
"How Frequently Do You Work on
Weekends?" by Organizational Level.**

	Top and Executive	Upper Management	Management	Professional
One weekend per month	29%	33%	37%	29%
Two weekends per month	21%	22%	24%	24%
Three weekends per month	13%	10%	6%	7%
Every weekend	17%	10%	7%	8%
I do not work weekends	20%	25%	26%	32%

and didn't go elsewhere for more pay or better benefits or to be treated better, the organization would take care of them for the rest of their lives. The idea was that the loyal employee would earn a good salary while they were working and would end up with a good retirement package. The presumption was that the organization would protect the interests of the employee because that was the agreement—as well as the right thing to do.

With the mass downsizings of the 1970s and 1980s, it became apparent that the implicit work contract was no longer in force. But this expired contract was what Silents, Early Boomers, and Late Boomers were used to and what they expected when they entered the workforce. Somewhere in the back of some people's minds is the idea that those rules should still apply, even if no one is living by them anymore.

Gen Xers didn't enter the workforce until well after the implicit contract was broken. They did not begin work with any (even implicit) expectation that it was in their best interest to stay loyal to an organization. In fact, their experiences watching the downsizings in the 1980s had taught them that loyalty was actually a trap—that they would be protecting themselves and possibly enhancing their career if they were always to keep an eye out for the next best thing.

Thus one explanation for the difference between conventional wisdom and what the data say is that the difference relates more to attitude than to substance. Younger people behave as loyally at work as do older people, but for the younger generations perhaps their behavior isn't about being loyal to an organization so much as about doing what is best for their careers—just as it is for the older generations. Consider the cases of John and James:

> John is in his 30s and had been doing well working at Company A. He held a critical position and was well respected. One day he walked in and turned in his resignation because he had taken a job at Company B. When asked why he was leaving, he said that he had an opportunity for learning and advancement at Company B that Company A couldn't match, though the salaries were about the same. Most of John's peers who heard about it shrugged and thought it was just the common behavior of going where the options are better. But the people in management who were now faced with the added work of finding someone to do his job for what they had paid him grumbled about a lack of loyalty. After all, he left *them* as much as he did the company, and if he were loyal, he would've stayed!

> James is in his early 50s and had been working for his company for about a decade. He had done a good job, but had plateaued. A headhunter called him and said there was a position at a start-up that would allow him more latitude and a potentially massive payout in stock options when the company went public. When James explained why he was leaving, no one said one word about his being disloyal. They thought he was making a good choice, given his opportunities at the new company. Although they were sad to lose his institutional knowledge, they could hire a new person at half his salary.

Reduced to its essentials, what typically happens is that younger people who leave for anything other than family reasons are spoken of as being disloyal or as crass opportunists (depending on what they're going to be doing), whereas older people who leave after having been around for many years are spoken of more kindly. Why is that? It is in part because there is still often the underlying assumption that younger people should be grateful for having a job at all, whereas older people have earned their positions—and their right to leave—through their tenure. If you believe that someone should be grateful for the position she holds (in essence, that she owes the company something because the company employs her), then you will be resentful of that person's leaving when she still "owes." If you believe that the (younger) individual does not owe the organization more than the organization owes her, then you'll be less likely to think of her as being disloyal.

We also hear people complaining about entitlement. We hear griping about how older employees act as if they are entitled to benefits in the workplace that no longer exist. They suggest that older employees don't understand that the world has changed since the 1950s and 1960s and that they can't expect to receive all the benefits they used to.

We also hear people saying that younger employees act as if they are entitled to special treatment at work. People say that younger employees expect to walk into the workplace and have everything the older ones have—immediately—without putting in the work that the older employees have to achieve at the same level. The implication is that younger people are spoiled rotten by their parents and schools and have no idea of what having a real job is like.

Although some of the criticism of both groups is undoubtedly reasonable, the use of the word "entitled" is inflammatory, and results in delegitimizing and belittling whatever group is being labeled. (It isn't clear that marginalizing the people the complaint is aimed at is always the intention when people say someone is acting entitled, but it is often the outcome.) To say that someone thinks she is entitled implies that she is trying to get something she doesn't deserve and is unwilling to work for. The crux of the issue is that people who complain about "disloyalty" and the "entitlement mentality" don't like feeling forced to give someone something they don't deserve—for whatever reason.

What employees are willing to accept and what employers have to offer to keep good employees are both largely driven by the economy rather than by perceptions of loyalty—or the lack of it. When a resource (good people to do the work) is scarce, it commands more from the marketplace (money, vacation time, respect, flexibility, and so on) than when the resource is plentiful. According to U.S. Bureau of Labor's *Monthly Labor Review* (Dohm, 2000;

"So, does anyone else feel that their needs aren't being met?"

Toosi, 2005), the dip in birth rates between the Baby Boom and its echo makes people born between about 1963 and 1980— Generation X—a relatively scarce commodity. As was the case for the Silent Generation and as is the case for Gen X, when there are too few people for the number of jobs available, employees can ask for more, and organizations have to offer more if they want to attract and keep employees—even relatively young, untrained employees.

Even though deep down, people of all generations don't necessarily think that being loyal in the old sense is good for their careers, our research shows that they behave as if they believe that hard work and not changing jobs too frequently are good for their careers. And if that isn't a concrete measure of loyalty today, we don't know what is.

Obviously these data show that people of all generations behave about the same way when it comes to concrete demonstrations of loyalty. What we also see is that people higher in organizations demonstrate more loyalty behaviors (working longer hours and more weekends) than do people lower in organizations. This makes sense, in that people higher up have more to gain by the success (and more to lose from the failure) of their organization. It is in their best interest to behave in a very loyal way . . . until they decide to leave and become loyal to their next organization.

It also makes sense that the people highest in organizations (who are generally older) would be complaining the most about the lack of loyalty to the organization. They demonstrate the behaviors that show loyalty—why doesn't everyone else?

The good news for organizations is that if managers can figure out a way to increase the loyalty of their older employees, it should work about as well with the younger ones. (We'll talk about different tactics managers can use later in this chapter.)

So it is about as easy to increase the loyalty of younger people as it is to increase the loyalty of those older workers who may have lived through (or witnessed) many downsizings. The reality is that loyalty as an expectation an organization has of its employees doesn't work unless the organization is willing to be equally loyal. What can an organization do to show loyalty to its workers? Increase their pay? Give them enough resources to do their job? Give them more days off so they can spend more time with their families? Have the highest ranks of the organization take a pay cut—rather than cut staff—when times are hard? The nature and scope of this book really don't allow us to go into detail here; we recommend that you read *Treat People Right!* by Edward Lawler III and *The Loyalty Effect* by Frederich Reichheld. Lawler's book gets right to the heart of what makes an organization worth being loyal to; Reichheld's yields insights about the topic of loyalty in general, which can be applied in many venues.

How This Applies to You

Even if people wanted to, the (unfortunate) truth is that they can't plan to stay with the same organization all their lives. There is too much churn in the system—too much outsourcing, too many layoffs, and too many mergers to make it likely that people will have the option to stay with one organization indefinitely. Therefore, they hedge their bets and work to make sure that they use available opportunities and get the development they need to stay a marketable product. This isn't disloyal; it is a rational response to a system that isn't going to take workers' personal needs and desires into account very often. Expecting to stay with one company for your whole working life and doing nothing to hedge against possible problems in the organization or the economy is roughly the equivalent of closing your eyes as you jaywalk across Broadway in Manhattan: you want to hope that everyone would stop for you, but you'll be more likely to survive if you keep an eye out for oncoming traffic . . . and be ready to run!

However, changing jobs when there isn't an unfixable problem isn't typically productive—unless you just like disruption in your life! If you aren't happy with your position, you'll want to think about a few questions while you're making your decisions:

- What exactly is it that you aren't happy about? (We mean specifically.) Is it the current project? When is it scheduled to end? Can you hang in there given an end date?
- Are you unhappy with your boss? Can you transfer to a different boss? How much longer will you be in this position reporting to this person? Can you think of a way to make working with the person more palatable? Perhaps you can make working with the person a learning experience for yourself. After all, the more people with whom you can work effectively, the better it is for your career!
- Do you feel as if you're stagnating in your job? Are you not learning? What do you want to learn? Can you set up a plan with your boss?
- Why do you think the new job would be better? What do you think you would get there that you aren't getting in your current position?
- Make a list of everything you like about your current job. Are you going to get the same things at the new job? What is going to be missing? What else do you think you're going to get?
- Make a list of everything you dislike about your current job. How many are big things, and how many are small annoyances? Of the big things, how many are going to disappear if

you take the other job? Are these large problems going to be fixed, or are new faces just going to be attached to the same problems? With regard to the small things, be specific about why you think you aren't going to have to deal with the same (or very similar) issues at the new organization.

Often the new job looks good just because it is different—after all, the grass really *does* seem greener on the other side of the fence! But is it actually greener? Sometimes people get so frustrated with their current situation that they just leave rather than work on the problem first. Although some problems can't be fixed, many can. And you have to think about whether—in the final analysis—you're going to gain more than a new desk and phone number if you change jobs. Consider Barb's story.

> Barb was so unhappy with her boss, Michael, that she was thinking about leaving her job. She said that Michael was irresponsible and annoying. He not only failed to do what he said he was going to do but also didn't require two people who reported to him to do their own work, which left three team members doing the work of the other two. Michael also had some personal behaviors (body language and tone of voice, for example) that constantly annoyed Barb. Barb was furious with his lack of follow-through—and was mentally finished with the job. Her colleagues on the team kept telling her that there were annoying coworkers and bosses everywhere, that just because she left this job didn't mean that the people at her next job were going to be any better—no matter how great they seemed during the interview. They reminded her that Michael had seemed to be great when he had interviewed, and look how he turned out. So Barb made a list of everything she liked about the job and everything she didn't like. She then thought about the things she didn't like, and determined which could be fixed, which couldn't, which might be better at another organization, and which would be likely to be worse. Currently she's still in her position.

What did Barb do about Michael? She went to his boss and asked for coaching on how to deal with Michael more effectively. She figured that even if his boss had no useful suggestions, she was forcing his boss to take the problem seriously. She also decided that she was going to change her attitude toward her interactions with Michael and not expect him to do what he said he was going to do. She believed that if she no longer expected him to follow through, she would be less bothered when he didn't and would be pleasantly surprised when he did. In this way she created a much happier environment for herself in her current job. She isn't completely happy, but she is happy enough to stay. Even better, she believes that she can learn a lot from dealing with the current situation and is sure that sticking this out will lead to a better position in the future.

Staying in a job isn't necessarily better for you than leaving. What is best for you is understanding exactly why you're making the decision you are making and what you expect to achieve by choosing the course you have. As long as you've thought that through, you've done all you can.

If You Are a Manager

One of the many difficult things managers have to deal with is employees leaving. Whether you're facing the loss of several employees or a single exceptional one, try to remember that their leaving isn't necessarily about a lack of loyalty. Some managers take an employee's leaving as an expression of disloyalty to them as people and as managers, and as a direct indictment—a personal insult. Although in some cases that assessment is probably fair (people tend to leave bosses at least as much as they do organizations), in many others it isn't.

As a manager, you would do well to assume that "it's not about you" and to try to determine why the person wants to leave. If it is something about his current position that needs to be fixed or something that he wants to learn, you might be able to take care of the problem. If someone is a good employee and is unhappy with something about the job, it is a good idea to listen and to try to fix the problem. Often people are even willing to wait if they're told that the problem will be taken care of. But beware of taking too long to fix the problem—the employee at some point will begin to believe that you are stringing him along and have no real interest in fixing the problem—and therefore no real investment in his best interests. At that point the employee is gone, and he's leaving with a bad taste in his mouth.

But if the employee just wants to go to learn something at a new organization (which is something he can't get if he stays with his current organization), then you know he is going to leave, and it is perhaps in your best interest to help him find another good job. After all, one of the best ways for organizations to attract new employees is for someone (current and past employees) to recommend them. People typically recommend organizations that they think treat employees well. What better PR for your organization than to help an employee find a good job somewhere else? By showing him that you respect him enough as a human being to want him to be happy, and helping him do something for himself that is theoretically against your best interest, you are earning this employee's enduring goodwill. And it helps if you tell him before he leaves that you want him to keep in touch and to be sure to check in when he's ready to change jobs again. Though you may have lost a good employee, he will undoubtedly say good things about you and your organization, is likely to recommend that other good people go work for the organization, and may even come back in the future because he was treated so well.

What You Should Have Learned from This Chapter

- Different generations have about the same levels of loyalty.
- Younger generations are not more likely to job-hop than older generations were at the same age.
- People who are closer to retirement are more likely to want to stay with the same organization for the rest of their working life.
- People higher in an organization work more hours than do people lower in the organization; working more isn't a matter of what generation an employee is from.

It's as Easy to Retain a Young Person as an Older One—If You Do the Right Things

As you've probably noticed by now, the principles in this book, though distinct and supported by their own data, do build on and overlap with one another. This chapter is no exception. Loyalty and retention are in many ways two sides of the same coin.

Nonetheless, the issue of retention does come with its own thorny set of generational assumptions (and resulting questions). We're sure that you've heard people complain about how difficult it is to retain good people. They complain that people leave for more money, leave to try something new, and leave because they're offered faster promotions. Much of the commentary we've heard focuses on how older people are much easier to retain than younger people because younger people are unreasonable in what they expect from a job. Consider the following situation:

> Ellen, employed as a consultant and officially identified by her organization as a high-potential employee, had been in the same job for three years and had begun to feel that she was stagnating. She did very well in the position, but she wasn't learning anything new. Because she liked the organization she was working for and didn't want to leave, she asked the PTBs (Powers That Be) in her organization for a transfer to another division. They told her they were willing to have her move; they just needed to find someone to replace her. She understood their position and didn't push the issue.
>
> After four months of no movement—and no one's being identified to go into her position—Ellen told them she really wanted the move and that if it

didn't happen, she was going to start looking for a job elsewhere. The PTBs told her she would have to be patient. They said she was young, that the move would happen eventually, and that in the meantime she should just be happy with the good job she was doing currently. She told them that if she didn't see real movement and decisions being made in two months, she would start looking elsewhere.

Three months later she accepted a position with another organization that would allow her the growth she wanted—as well as pay her 30% more than her old salary. The PTBs were horrified and wondered what her problem was—after all, they had said they were working on it; what else did she want from them? Privately, she said what she wanted was something *done,* not just talked about endlessly. To her it was obvious that the PTBs didn't take either her or her request seriously, or they would've done something. So *she* did something. They lost an excellent employee, and she got paid a lot more to learn and become a more valuable employee.

Why did the organization lose Ellen? Because keeping her didn't matter enough to the PTBs for them to do something about it. The executives said, after the fact, that she had been too impatient and that moving her wasn't a high priority for the organization.

Two of the primary reasons organizations are interested in generational differences are concerns about bench strength and succession planning. Leaders understand that they need people to run the organization after they've retired. They also understand that they can't hire these individuals at the last minute—that some of those who will be running the organization in 10 years need to be developed within the organization over time. The problem leaders are stuck with is retention: keeping the people they want to keep.

There are currently two major issues with retention. One relates to the population and economy, the other to culture. The population issue (also mentioned in the previous chapter) is that there were fewer people born between 1964 and 1982 (Generation X) than there were between 1946 and 1963 (the Baby Boom). So as the Baby Boom retires, and Generation X moves up the ladder into age-appropriate positions, there are going to be more positions open and fewer people to fill them. Since there are fewer appropriate candidates to hire, and more open positions to fill, the candidates will have more—and better—options.

For organizations, this translates into the "war for talent" (Michaels, Handfield-Jones, and Axelrod, 2001). Organizations have to do more than just provide a job if they want to keep the best employees.

> Not only will companies have to devise more imaginative hiring practices; they will also have to work harder to keep their best people. . . . A lot of it has to do with demographics. In 15 years [about 2012], there will be 15% fewer Americans in the 35- to 45-year-old range than there are now. At the same time, the U.S. economy is likely to grow at a rate of 3% to 4% per year. So over that period, the demand for bright, talented 35- to 45-year-olds will increase by, say, 25%, and the supply will be going down by 15%. That sets the stage for a talent war [Fishman, 1998, p. 104].

One option organizations exercise is to try to keep retiring workers around as long as they can so that there will be enough people with enough knowledge to do the work. Another option is to try to develop new employees faster. A third way organizations deal with the shortfall is to outsource some of the work. In some cases outsourcing backfires because it causes some employees to think that their jobs aren't stable, so they look for work elsewhere.

As we discussed in the chapter on loyalty, there has been a change in the implicit employment contract in the past 30 years, such that there is no longer an understanding that if you (as an employee) do a good job and don't mess up big time or harass people, your employer will keep you around indefinitely. People now presume that their organization may lay them off at any time in one of the cyclical downsizings we all read about in the news. Organizations bemoan the lack of loyalty in workers today, but most are unwilling to provide the assurance necessary to keep people loyal.

The unintended consequence of this situation is that people now feel as if they are working within a free agency system (to borrow a term from professional sports). In other words, each "player" (employee) can look for the best deal for herself rather than think first and foremost about what is good for the "team." (There might not be an "I" in "team," but there is an "I" in "win," and even in "survive.") What else can a person do when she thinks she's likely to be laid off with only minimal severance at a moment's notice?

The smaller pool of workers to choose from and the prevalence of the free agency system have made retention a bigger issue with organizations than leaders remember it having been in the

"We expect little loyalty. In return, we offer little security."

past. Executives talk about "bench strength" issues and say, "We can't develop leaders for the organization because we can't seem to keep the people we want to keep." And typically they say that people are leaving out of simple greed, which management supposedly can't do anything about, so it is out of their hands. But is that an accurate assessment of the situation? Are employees' requests so unreasonable that an organization can't be expected to pay attention to them? Is money truly the bottom line for people looking for other jobs, or are other issues equally important?

To address this question, as part of our study we asked people, What does your organization need to do to retain you as a committed employee?

Research

We received 2,732 responses to our question. Silents made up 8% of the responses, 28% came from Early Boomers, 30% from Late Boomers, 30% from Early Xers, and 4% from Late Xers. Figures 8.1 and 8.2 illustrate the responses sorted by generation and by organizational level, respectively.

Figure 8.1. Responses to the Question, "What Does Your Organization Need to Do to Retain You as a Committed Employee?" by Generation.

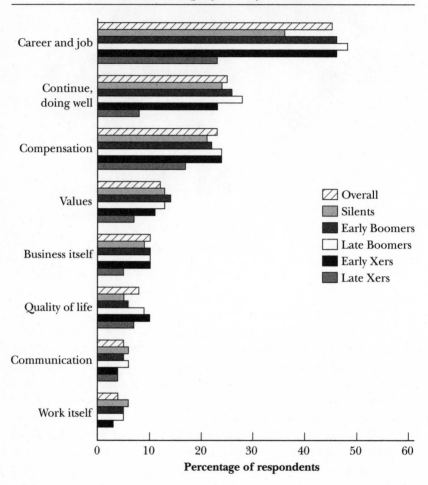

The primary categories of responses, in order of frequency, were as follows:

- *Issues with the career and job:*

  - *Advancement and opportunity.* Desire for advancement, upward mobility, growth in position, changing roles, and promotion.
  - *Learning, development, challenge.* Wants to be kept challenged, interested, engaged, motivated, and energized through

Figure 8.2. Responses to the Question, "What Does Your Organization Need to Do to Retain You as a Committed Employee?" by Organizational Level.

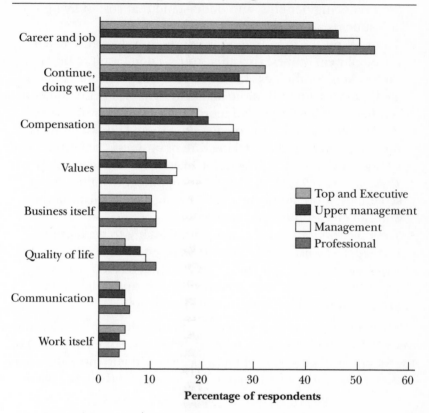

education, training, on-the-job learning, or any other venue. Asks for increased responsibility.

○ *Respect, recognition, acknowledgment, appreciation.* Appreciation for rewards in other forms besides pay.

○ *Resources, other support.* Demand to have what is needed to do the work (including the resources or technology I need to be effective).

• *Continue.* The organization should keep doing what it's doing and let me keep doing what I'm doing. This category also included positive statements that indicated that people's needs were currently being met.

- *Better compensation.* Including higher salary, better benefits, bigger bonus, better perks, bigger pension, more school reimbursement, pay for school or training, more stock options. Stop reducing benefits, and understand that cost of living adjustments aren't enough of a "reward."
- *Values.* Wants the organization to express its values and match the employees' values. (In other words, I don't want to find out I'm working for the next Enron.) Specific requests for better organizational standards, more and better vision, a better job environment, and less stress and more creativity in the workplace.
- *The business itself.* What the organization should do as a business or organization, including "taking care of business," organizational change, innovation, and better management and leadership.
- *Better quality of life.* Desire for balance, time, flexibility, better schedules, more family time, more holiday and vacation time, and the opportunity to take the time.
- *Better communication.* Included people asking to be kept informed, to be listened to, and to be given feedback.
- *Improvements to the work itself.* These included references to a desire for more autonomy, control, input, authority, and a greater contribution within their specific job.

Because many responses covered more than one topic, they were often coded into more than one category. For example, all of the following responses would have been coded into more than one category, because each of them talks about more than one issue:

> Keep good benefits [and] health insurance,
> and improve pay and appreciation.
> —Silent

> Pay me, train me, offer interesting work.
> —Early Boomer

> Provide some sort of rewards (that is, monetary,
> travel, added responsibilities) for a job well done.
> —Late Boomer

> Offer challenging positions/projects;
> remain competitive with market salaries.
> —Early Xer

> Ask for and listen to my input, and
> compensate my work with adequate pay.
> —Late Xer

Research Note

As part of the research process, there are a number of ways to go about coding comments. Some researchers read through the comments and look for themes and leave it at that. They make no attempt to count how frequently people mention a particular issue; instead, they guess which comments are made more frequently than others. The problem with that method is that it is prone to memory error: we are more likely to remember those responses we expected and those we agree with, and are less likely to remember responses we disagree with or didn't expect.

Another way researchers code these types of responses is to have a preset list of categories and code the responses into those categories—and anything that doesn't fit those categories is ignored. In this method, researchers have already decided what the options are, and cannot identify anything that is inconsistent with what they expected to find. This method is much more likely to give you the answer you are looking for, rather than the real answer, because it has not left any place for the surprises that always come with good research. Well-trained researchers can always set up research to give them the answer they want—it is more difficult to set up research so that you can find out what you don't already know!

What we did was to have two people read through about 30% of the responses and look for themes. We put these themes into categories, such as Career and Compensation, and then went through coding each comment by what its theme was. We also double-checked about 30% of the coding every 200 responses to make sure we were coding consistently. After we did that, we looked at all responses by theme and created subcategories to identify what aspect of the greater theme the person was talking about (for example, identifying Bonus as a subcategory of Compensation). Thus the results you see reported here are a combination of our letting the data show us what the categories should be and a rigorous coding process by which we identified the theme (or themes!) of each of the comments.

It's as Easy to Retain a Young Person as an Older One—If You Do the Right Things

Overall, we find that people of all generations have the same ideas about what their organization can do to retain them. People are concerned primarily about their career, job, and compensation. A large number of people (25% of the total) are reasonably content—they simply said their organization should continue doing what it is already doing.

Compensation: It's Not Just About the Money

Yes, many people did say that compensation is a primary issue (see Figure 8.3): overall, 23% of the respondents mentioned compensation. But the comments weren't just about salary; they went beyond the actual cash in the paycheck. People of all generations and all levels also talked about bonuses, benefits (as separate from salary), and their pension or retirement plan. Interestingly, there were no generational differences in type of compensation mentioned; that is, older people did not focus more on benefits and retirement, or younger people on cash and bonuses. People of all generations focused equally on the different types of compensation. What this means for an organization is that it needs to realize that many younger employees are thinking almost as much about their retirement plans as older ones are, and older employ-

Figure 8.3. Percentage of Comments About Compensation Coming from Each Generation.

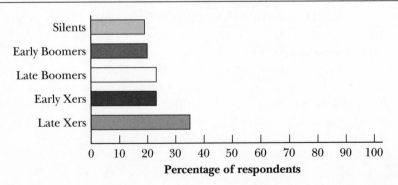

ees are just as concerned with their base salary and bonuses as younger ones are.

We also found that comments about compensation don't come just from the lower levels in the organization—people in the executive ranks were dissatisfied as well. (Figure 8.4 compares organizational levels in terms of number of comments about compensation.) So it isn't just the greedy, high-powered younger people who aren't happy with their compensation.

Career Issues

Within the career and job category, the responses were in the areas of learning, development, and challenge; advancement and opportunity; and respect and recognition. (Figures 8.5 and 8.6 illustrate the responses sorted by generation and by organizational level, respectively.) In the next sections, we'll look at these responses in terms of the individual generations.

Silent Generation

With regard to retaining Silents, learning, development, and challenge and respect and recognition were more important than resources or advancement and opportunity. People from the Silent generation want to continue to learn and develop and want challenge in their job. They are not interested in sitting around and

Figure 8.4. Percentage of Comments About Compensation Coming from Each Level in the Organization.

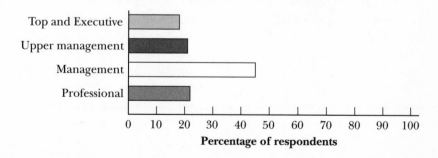

**Figure 8.5. Responses Within the Career
and Job Category, by Generation.**

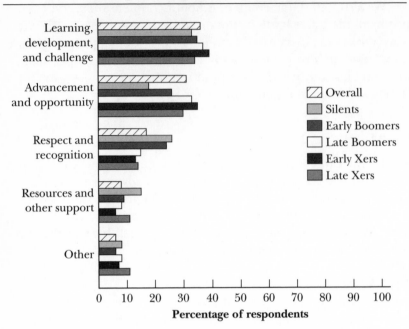

stagnating, being RIP (Retired in Position); they want to keep
learning and being challenged.

> Keep letting me learn new things.
> —Silent

It is also important to people from the Silent Generation that
they receive respect and recognition for the work they have done
and for what they know. To them, the issue of respect and recognition is second only to learning and is definitely more important
than either advancement and opportunity or resources. Silents feel
that they have contributed a great deal, and many of the respondents said that they didn't feel they received adequate recognition
for what they have contributed.

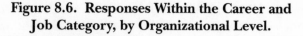

Figure 8.6. Responses Within the Career and Job Category, by Organizational Level.

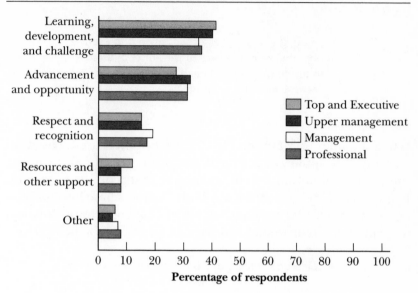

Respect experience rather than "young visionaries."
—Silent

Accept my entire career as one of high quality performance and contribution and recognize that I have served the organization beyond expectations and it is legitimate for senior professionals to pursue their interests and contribute in ways that challenge and reward them even when they are not fully congruent with what the organization expects of less experienced employees. In other words acknowledge that senior people are different.
—Silent

Although advancement and opportunity were mentioned less frequently by Silents, it was still an important category for them. People from this generation indicated that they were interested in advancing, though it wasn't as much of a focus as it was for people from other generations. When advancement was mentioned, it was often in the context of wanting new challenges and not wanting to feel stuck anymore.

> Promote me to a higher level position or present
> an opportunity for a lateral move—after 5–6 years
> in the same position I need something new.
> —Silent

Early Boomers

When it comes to retaining them, Early Boomers are focused on learning, development, and challenge more than they are on anything else, with advancement and opportunity coming in second. Being later in their careers, many Early Boomers have been in positions for a while and are ready for a new challenge. Early Boomers don't just want to sit around and stagnate for the rest of their careers.

> Offer continued training and professional development.
> —Early Boomer

> Offer a promotional opportunity or increase salary.
> —Early Boomer

> Provide an environment where opportunities for
> advancement are offered regardless of age.
> —Early Boomer

Early Boomers are almost as focused on respect and recognition as Silents are. Like the Silents, many Early Boomers feel that they are not as appreciated in their jobs as they should be, and they say that more respect and recognition for the work they are doing would make them much more likely to stay with the organization.

> Respect me as an individual and a professional.
> —Early Boomer

> Recognize and reward my contributions, although
> the recognition is probably more important.
> —Early Boomer

Opportunities for Advancement

Respondents expressed concern about being offered—or not being offered—opportunities for advancement—because of their age. Some of the older employees said they were being overlooked because they are older, and their employers aren't sure how much longer they're going to be around or whether it's worth investing in older workers to get them to the next level.

Some of you may think that it sounds reasonable not to invest in older workers because they won't be around as long, but this is a bad idea for two reasons. First, it is illegal to discriminate against older employees. Second, if you have no idea how long you're going to be able to keep a younger employee, why are they a better bet? Research shows that people stay with organizations longer as they get older because they are more settled in their communities and, because they have a better idea of what they like to do, have ended up in jobs that are more consistent with their interests. You actually might do as well investing in older employees as in younger ones.

Late Boomers

This group is more focused on learning, development, and challenge and on advancement and opportunity than they are on anything else. To retain the Late Boomers, an organization needs to focus on providing adequate development, making sure the employee is challenged, helping the employee figure out what he or she needs to advance within the organization, and helping the employee make or find opportunities for advancement.

> Provide continued professional learning and development opportunities.
> —Late Boomer

Late Boomers are less focused on respect and recognition than the older generations are, though it is still important to them. Late

Boomers want respect and recognition for what they do, but opportunities to advance within the organization, new challenges, and additional development may be just the recognition this generation needs. After all, a promotion is a great indication that you are respected and that your work is recognized.

Early Xers

This group responds almost identically to Late Boomers. They want respect and recognition, but they are much more focused on learning, developing, facing new challenges, and having the opportunity to advance within their organization. Retention strategies for Early Xers should focus on these areas. It is a good idea to check in with Early Xers to make sure that they feel challenged and don't feel they are stagnating on the job. They like continuous learning and dislike the feeling of running in place so much that they are likely to start looking for another job if they feel as if they aren't getting anywhere.

> Provide me with chances to learn more.
> —Early Xer

> Recognize work efforts and reward accordingly.
> —Early Xer

> Appreciate me for the work that I do and
> advance me accordingly so that I can grow.
> —Early Xer

> I would need to see a clear career path and
> opportunities for promotion and growth.
> —Early Xer

> Provide an interesting and challenging role that gives
> me a defined career path with transferable skills.
> —Early Xer

Late Xers

This group responds very similarly to Late Boomers and Early Xers. Late Xers are focused more on learning, developing, receiving more challenging assignments, and finding opportunities for advancement within the organization than they are on anything else. At the same time, Late Xers would also appreciate respect and recognition for the work they do.

> Offer and support continuing education.
> —Late Xer

> Allow me to move up within the organization
> and not let my age be a detriment.
> —Late Xer

> Reward good work more than seniority.
> —Late Xer

What about organizational level?

Overall, people at different organizational levels had the same priorities when it comes to retention issues. The only small difference of interest was that people at the top and executive levels and at the upper management level were more strongly focused on learning, development, and challenge as retention issues than were people from the management and professional levels.

Life Beyond Work

One of the categories of comments that appeared repeatedly as both a quality-of-life issue and a career issue was the organization's attitude toward the employee's life outside work. (Figure 8.7 shows the percentage of each generation who named quality of life as a primary career issue.) Some employees said they felt their organizations had forgotten that they had a life outside work or thought that the employee's life outside work was more of a hindrance or interference in what should be the individual's real priority—work. More than 200 people expressed concern about their work-life balance. Although people from all generations thought that work-life balance was an issue that had a significant impact on whether they were willing to stay with an organization, Late Boomers and Early Xers said this more often than other generations did, as did people who identified themselves as professionals in their organization.

Figure 8.7. Percentage of Respondents Who Named Quality of Life as a Primary Career Issue, by Generation.

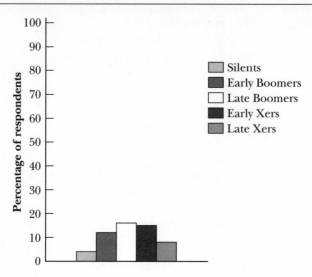

Care about my quality of life.
—Late Boomer

Many people said they would be more likely to stay with their organization if they could work on a flexible schedule. Younger people often said that they wanted flexible schedules because they had young children. They said they would get more work done and life would be more convenient for their families if they had a more flexible schedule. Many older people said that because they were close to retirement, they thought that a flexible schedule would be more convenient for them during this period. One suggestion was that offering a flexible schedule was a sign of the respect the organization had for its employees. If the employee does a good job and gets her work done, does it matter exactly when she does it?

Allow me to step down into a less demanding and
stressful position and perhaps work a 4-day workweek.
—Silent

Increase flexibility in work schedules and locations.
—Early Boomer

> Understand that my family commitments come
> first and allow flexibility in my hours of work.
> —Late Boomer

> Offer flexible work hours.
> —Early Xer

> Show commitment to allowing employees
> to focus on other aspects of their life.
> —Late Xer

Many people of all generations requested telecommuting as a work option because it allowed them more flexible schedules. They said the telecommuting option would make them more likely to stay with their organization because they saw it as being respectful of their home life. Many people talked about how telecommuting would reduce terrible daily commutes, which would result in their being more productive at work and better able to use their time with their families.

> Allow more staff members to telecommute.
> —Silent

> Allow flexibility in work schedules . . . possibly
> telecommuting a day or two a week as an option.
> —Early Boomer

People of all generations said they want to do a good job at work, but they also want to have a good quality of life, which work often hampered. Early Boomers, Late Boomers, and Early Xers talked about the quality-of-life issue more frequently than did Silents and Late Xers. Contrary to the conventional wisdom that says Xers are the ones constantly complaining about balance and quality of life, Late Boomers mentioned these topics as often as Early Xers did, and Early Boomers mentioned them almost as frequently.

People said that they want to do a good job at home and that work often interfered to the point that they had trouble figuring out their priorities. Some talked about how at work everything was deemed urgent—they were always having to put out fires—and how difficult it was to give higher priority to time with their family when feeling pressure to take care of an urgent work problem.

They said that this wouldn't be as much of an issue if everything at work weren't urgent. Some of the respondents talked about the difficulties of raising young families while in jobs that required extensive work in the evenings. Others talked about increased responsibilities for elderly parents that restrict the time they can work beyond standard hours.

What many respondents said was that there is too much work to be done during normal work hours, so people feel they have to work extra hours to make sure the work is done. They said they feel forced to decide what isn't going to get done or what they are going to do as substandard work so as to ensure that they have the necessary time with their families. They said that if the actual resources necessary to do the work were allocated, there wouldn't be these issues. But in their opinion their organizations don't care enough about their employees to bother with actually resourcing the work appropriately.

Many of the comments also included references to extreme stress. People talked about how the lack of resources combined with their wanting to do a good job for the client or organization results in their having had to take on a disproportionate amount of the stress. Some respondents said they were so disgusted with the situation that they had decided to deal with it by choosing to take a lower-level position in their organization.

> I have recently voluntarily stepped down from an upper
> management position. I am very happy with much less stress.
> —Early Boomer

> Do I accept the less stressful job for less pay or go back
> into industry and management for a higher salary?
> —Early Boomer

Some also talked about having to think about whether they would be able to have a life outside work if they were to accept a promotion. They said they wanted the new position, the new work, the new paycheck, and the learning that comes along with the new job, but they don't want their life to be engulfed by their work. They said they were torn between the job they wanted that would challenge them, and the kind of life they wanted to lead.

Many employees indicated that their organizations would need to stop trying to encroach on their nonwork time, or they would leave the organization for one that had more (apparent) respect for them. People said they often felt that their organizations treated them like cogs in a machine. They said their organizations looked on their life outside work as a necessary evil rather than as an important part of their life.

> They must stop pushing so hard for the "bold goal"
> and understand that people have lives outside of work.
> —Early Xer

When Nothing Is Going to Help

It is apparent from the comments we received that there are some people who can't be retained short of tripling their pay or stapling them to their chairs. (We are not advocating for that solution.) A few people of all generations said there was nothing their organization could do to retain them.

MANKOFF

*"Quit complaining. In these times, most people would
be happy to have your job security."*

The most common reason people from the older generations (especially the Silents) gave for leaving was retirement. Retaining potential retirees can be a competitive advantage for organizations because these employees are already knowledgeable, need little training, and can often fill in part-time.

Many of the respondents who said they were thinking about re-tiring mentioned that they would be willing to stay at their orga-nization in return for a few accommodations, including part-time work, flexible schedules, and adequate compensation. Given the number of people who are likely to retire in the next ten years, and the impending shortage of younger people with the right knowl-edge and experience to replace them, keeping people as part-time employees who are retiring could turn out to be a competitive ad-vantage for those organizations who do it effectively. After all, why not keep all of that valuable knowledge around if you can!

Younger people said they were leaving primarily because they didn't see adequate opportunities for advancement or learning in their organization. They were concerned that their career was going to stagnate, and many of them thought they would need to leave their organization to prevent that from happening. These people also said that their organization could retain them if it were willing to work with them and give them more opportunities. But they seemed to think that this was unlikely to happen.

> Offer me continued opportunities for learning and travel.
> Appreciate the time and energy I put into work, and
> reward me appropriately. But eventually I will want to
> work for a larger organization, so I will leave.
> —Early Xer

Some of the people who said that their organization couldn't retain them said they were looking for opportunities that weren't available in their current organization. Their wanting to leave wasn't about disliking the organization or the people they work with, but rather about wanting to broaden their experience. Leav-ing to get experience in a different organization (smaller or larger) or in a different industry is common, and can be used to the ad-vantage of the organization the person is leaving (more on this in the next section).

If You Are a Manager

People of all generations said they wanted the same things:

- Opportunity to advance within their organization
- Learning and development
- Respect and recognition
- Better quality of life
- Better compensation

What this means is that you should be asking not what you can do to retain younger employees but what you can do to retain employees of any generation. An organization that wants to retain people should focus on four areas.

1. *An organization should have a plan in place to help people at all levels and of all generations understand how they can move within the organization.* Even people nearing retirement didn't want to feel stuck in one job or position; they too wanted the opportunity to advance or change jobs. Although people were very interested in the opportunity to advance, typically they didn't say that the organization had to advance them, just that they wanted the opportunity to advance. It was apparent from the comments that one of the reasons so many people were focusing on advancement was that they wanted a tangible expression of respect and recognition for their work, which they didn't feel they were currently getting. Some say that the only way they can know whether they are respected is through tangibles; they take good pay, good benefits, time off, and a more family-friendly environment as indications that the organization has respect for them. They also say that the opportunity to advance within their organization and access to learning and development are indications that the organization respects employees' contributions and acknowledges their value to the organization.

2. *An organization should have a plan in place to help people get the development they need so that they can grow in their position.* Organizations can help employees set up learning plans that correspond to what the employee wants to do next. (Remember: whatever their

generation, people want to do *something* next.) In addition to what the employee is going to learn and where he is going to apply it, the learning plan should include a commitment from the organization about what time it is going to provide to the individual for his learning, what portion of the learning it is going to pay for, and what support it is going to provide to the employee so that he isn't trying to learn in addition to doing all of his other standard work.

3. *An organization should review its compensation policy.* If it isn't possible to increase the compensation of those who are really not paid well, the organization could look at increasing vacation days or other paid time off. Our results indicate that quality of life is so important to people that having more (paid) time off with their families might be an acceptable trade-off for additional cash.

In many of the comments, people suggested that the opportunity for advancement would also be an acceptable trade-off for not increasing pay. Other people said the opposite: that they have no chance of advancement in their current situation, but would be willing to stay anyway if the salary were increased.

4. *An organization should make an effort—a real, honest, concerted effort—to recognize the good work each employee does.* Some employees feel most recognized when the recognition is given in a public forum. Others see public "recognition days" as just another example of corporate PR being done to raise morale and therefore as manipulative BS. (In other words, public recognition makes these employees feel even worse than they did before, because they see it as blatant manipulation and therefore inherently disrespectful.) So in some cases recognition is best done personally, by someone who works with and knows the employee well. This is definitely a situation where there is no one-size-fits-all solution.

Although younger and older people want the same things at work, they don't always want them in the same amounts. For example, older people may be more focused on respect and recognition, whereas younger people may be more focused on learning and moving up the ladder. But if older and younger people want the same things from their organization, why is it that people think that younger employees are more difficult to retain than older ones are? In part because younger employees *do* change jobs more frequently than older ones do. If you think back to Principle 7 (Loyalty Depends on the Context, Not on the Generation), you'll remember that we presented data about how frequently people said they changed jobs at different ages. They reported that they changed jobs more frequently when they were younger than they did when they were older. According to our data, that was as true 40 years ago as it is today. What is happening is that people who notice the difference in frequency attribute it to generation. They think the difference is new because they don't remember thinking that there was anything wrong with how frequently they changed jobs when they were that age. They think that younger people must want something very different from their employers. The reality is that younger people's changing jobs is not new, nor does it indicate that younger employees want radically different things from older ones.

So why is it that younger employees leave more frequently than older ones do? There are a few primary factors. One is that younger people are typically at an earlier career stage than are older people, which means that they are still figuring out what they really like doing. One way they do that is by trying new jobs, either within an organization or (when an organization isn't willing to move people around) by changing employers. Much of this learning can be done within an organization if managers understand that young people's desire to change jobs relatively frequently isn't necessarily a result of a short attention span, but rather comes out of a desire to learn what the best fit is for them.

Another reason younger people leave more frequently is that they are less likely than older people are to own homes or to have spouses and children. If they aren't as tied to the area, they are more likely to be willing to leave to get what they want in a job, and therefore they are more likely to do so.

It is interesting to note that almost everything the respondents asked for and said would keep them with their organization was possible for their organizations to do. (The requests were possible; whether they were reasonable is a judgment call.) What quickly became apparent to us is that retaining people isn't terribly difficult if an organization is willing to take concrete action. The issue appears to be that organizations rarely do anything that employees explicitly recognize as an effort to retain them.

Employees want to feel that they are valued at work. They want to feel that their needs are a priority for someone. Although the idea might seem paradoxical, another way to convey the same sentiment is to say that employees want to feel that they are making a valuable contribution at work. In many cases, being needed and having one's needs met are closely related.

Some of the survey respondents indicated that more money, regardless of other factors, will keep them loyal to a job for some time. But organizations have to be careful with this option; buying loyalty can have implications beyond the immediate benefit of keeping people in their positions. For example, who *isn't* getting the raise? Even if you try to prevent discussion and comparison of compensation packages, you know that people talk with each other and find out if someone in the same position is getting a better deal. Employees do in fact get raises (and other perks) when they come in with an offer letter from another company (what people used to call "telegram-waving"). But how does this make their peers feel? Unfortunately, getting some people to stay by paying them more may have an unintended adverse effect on the whole group.

What should you do if there is someone whom you really want to keep but who you know is going to leave no matter what? Why not tell the person how great you think she is, and how impressive it is that she is taking control of her own development and career? As we discussed in the chapter on loyalty, why not tell her that she should call you in a few years to discuss coming back to the organization? Even if she never calls, she will leave feeling that you respect her and appreciate her talent and contribution. An employee leaving with a good impression of the organization (and of you as someone in that organization) can do nothing but good things for your reputation as a boss and for the reputation of your organization as a place that respects and appreciates talent.

If You Are an Employee on the Verge of Changing Jobs

If you are an employee who is increasingly dissatisfied at work, there are a few things you need to think about. You might even want to write down your thoughts—sometimes forcing yourself to write everything down makes the situation clearer.

- What exactly is it that you aren't happy about? Be specific.

  - Is your boss the problem? If so, can you move to report to someone else?

- ○ Do you feel as if work that used to be interesting is now boring because you're not learning anything? Is there really nothing else to learn on the job? What can you do so that you can learn more? Do you know what you need to be learning to make the next move in your career?
- ○ Do you feel that your organization doesn't appreciate your contribution? Frankly, this is common. Do you feel that your boss doesn't appreciate your contribution? Do you think he means to be giving you that message, or is it that he's just really busy and hasn't thought about it? Do you feel that your peers appreciate you? What about your direct reports? What would people need to be doing to make you feel appreciated?
- ○ Is the compensation inadequate? We're not talking inadequate as in "less that you'd like" (we'd *all* like to make more—even if we already make a ton); we're talking about inadequate as in "My quality of life is seriously damaged by what I'm being paid." For some people, compensation has to do with basic survival and paying their bills. For others, making more money is a tangible reflection of how much their organization values their contribution. You need to decide what compensation means to you and exactly how important it is.

- Why do you think the new job would be better?

  - ○ What do you think you would get there that you aren't getting in the current position? Are you sure you'll get it?
  - ○ Make a list of everything you like about your current job. Are you going to get the same things at the new job? What is going to be missing? What additional things do you think you're going to get that are going to make you happier there than you are here?
  - ○ Make a list of everything you dislike about your current job. How many are big things, and how many are small annoyances?

    Of the big things, how many are going to disappear if you take the other job? Are these large problems going to be fixed, or are new faces just going to be attached to the same problems?

> With regard to the small things, be specific about why you
> think you aren't going to have to deal with the same (or
> very similar) issues at the new organization.

Sometimes people get so frustrated with their current situation
that they leave rather than try to fix the problem first. Although
some problems can't be fixed, many can. And you have to think
about whether, in the final analysis, you're going to gain more than
a new desk and phone number if you change jobs. Sometimes you
definitely will. Other times—six months after you've changed
jobs—you'll realize that the problems are at least as bad as at the
last place; you just have them in a different building. What you
need to do is understand what is motivating your decision (for example, what you expect to achieve by making that decision) and
be realistic about what changing jobs is going to do for you in the
short and long run.

Let's return to Ellen's story.

What Ellen wanted was very similar to what the survey respondents said they
wanted—for the organization to respect her enough to help her learn. She
was willing to stay with this organization, where she felt she was underpaid,
because she valued the additional developmental opportunities she thought
she could get there. When the organization did nothing to help her, Ellen left.
From her perspective, what else could she do?

Of course, there was something the organization could've done. Did the
PTBs truly feel that they had done enough to let Ellen know that she was
needed and valued? And did the organization want her to stay? Think back to
the tenor of the comments the PTBs made after she left. Was she truly a valued
employee?

If she were truly valued, there were certainly other avenues to pursue. For
one, the PTBs could have been more forthcoming regarding timing, available
opportunities, and the process of finding a replacement. For another, they
could have offered to increase significantly the scope and depth of Ellen's job
even if an immediate transfer was not possible.

Ellen's perception was that she was running into more of a political problem than a functional one. She felt that the people whom she was asking to
move her thought that she had more of an obligation to the organization than
the organization had to her—in other words, that she should be happy with

what she was getting and shut up about it, that she would get what she asked for when it was convenient for the organization (and the PTBs) and not as a response to her needs. They never explicitly told her that, but when she discussed the issue with them, their attitude seemed to be along the lines of "This isn't convenient for us right now, so you'll just have to wait. And if you push it you're behaving like a spoiled brat, because you should be grateful that you have a good job." Ellen felt as though her (reasonable) needs were at the bottom of the PTBs' priority list—not a pleasant feeling—so she left.

Ellen could have gone back to the PTBs yet again and asked for a change. But in truth, she felt she had done enough: she had been a good employee by telling them about the issue many times and giving them ample time (six months) to come to a mutually agreeable solution. She felt that their inaction indicated that they were unacceptably taking her for granted, so it was in her best interest to go elsewhere. It turns out that she was paid 30% more in her new job and given ample opportunities for learning.

We wish we could say that the PTBs learned from this experience and started paying attention when younger employees expressed these kinds of concerns, but they haven't. Happily, many organizations do not have these same failings—and those organizations benefit!

What You Should Have Learned from This Chapter

- Employees of all generations are more likely to remain with an organization if they receive

  Good compensation
  Learning and development
  Opportunities for advancement
  Respect and recognition
  Good quality of life outside work

- Employers can focus their efforts on this list (above), but must realize that each individual wants a slightly different combination of compensation, learning, advancement, quality of life, and respect.
- Just about everyone feels underpaid and overworked—including me!

Everyone Wants to Learn— More Than Just About Anything Else

In the previous chapter, we explained that retaining good employees, for all generations, has as much to do with learning and development as it does with making a lot of money. In this chapter we talk about what our research revealed about learning—what people want to learn, how they want to learn, and how organizations can meet those needs.

In our survey, learning and development were among the issues brought up the most frequently by people of all generations. Some people told us that the younger generations don't want to learn because they think they already know everything. (Seriously, everything.) Others said that older people don't want to learn because they think they already know everything. Somehow it is comforting that people have the same complaints about younger and older people!

Across the board, however, people talked and talked and talked about how central they thought learning and development were for their careers. They also talked about learning and development being important retention factors and about how they were likely to look elsewhere if they felt that they weren't getting enough (or the right kind) of development in their current position.

We asked people to answer a number of questions about learning and development in the workplace. Overall,

- 90% of respondents said that they were learning on the job.
- 79% said that they are developing the skills they need for the future.

- 63% said they believe that their organization will develop them as an employee.
- 97% said that it was important for them to learn on the job. (And how often do 97% of people agree on anything?)

These results held for people of all generations.

Research

Overall, 21% of people of all generations volunteered comments about the importance of learning and development for their advancing within the organization and were concerned about what they need to learn and how they're going to learn it. Because people of all generations think that learning is critically important, we felt that organizations would benefit from learning more about the kinds of developmental opportunities and learning methods employees prefer. So we focused our research on these questions:

What do people want to learn? Does it differ by generation or level in the organization?

How do people want to learn?

What People Want to Learn

Overall, the following are the top ten areas in which people intend to get training:

1. Leadership
2. Skills training in their field of expertise
3. Team building
4. Problem solving and decision making
5. Strategic planning
6. Managing change
7. Computer training
8. Vision
9. Communication skills
10. Conflict management

As you see, leadership came in at the top of the list, with skills training shortly behind it. (See Table 9.1 for the complete list of

Table 9.1. Percentage of Respondents Saying They Intend to Get Development in Each Area in the Next Year.

Areas of Development	Overall (%)
Leadership	79
Skills training in my field of expertise	74
Team building	68
Problem solving, decision making	65
Strategic planning	59
Managing change	58
Computer training	57
Vision	56
Communication skills	54
Conflict management	53
Management and business skills	53
Performance appraisal	50
Self-awareness	50
Quality and process improvement	49
Public speaking and presentation skills	47
Career coaching skills	45
Diversity	43
Time management	42
Career planning	40
Diplomacy and politics at work	39
Creativity	39
Other	39
Life balance	37
Hiring, interviewing	33
Ethics	33
International customs, cultural adaptability	25
Foreign language	23
International business knowledge	21
Entrepreneurialism	21
Sales	12

skills respondents reported intending to learn.) Skills involved in being a good leader (team building, problem solving and decision making, strategic planning, managing change, vision, communication skills, and conflict management) also showed up in the top ten. People of all generations want assistance in learning how to be better leaders. Many feel that they have a good handle on how to do the technical and administrative aspects of the job, but they believe they could use more help with the "people" aspects. It is therefore reasonable that people skills end up at the top of the development list.

Computer training also shows up in the top ten. The fact that technology is always changing (for better or for worse), causing organizations to frequently upgrade their hardware and software, means that people are constantly in need of training on the new equipment. People understand that they will do their job most efficiently if they don't have to spend a lot of time arguing with (or swearing at!) their computers.

Standard business skills start to show up in the next five (management and business skills, performance appraisal, quality and process improvement), indicating that people would appreciate more standard business and project management training in addition to the leadership training that tops their list.

Going Global?

Considering the pervasive impact of globalization, it is surprising and sad that international business skills, such as international customs, cultural adaptability, foreign language, and international business knowledge, were at the bottom of the list of desired developmental areas. Given the increasingly global nature of work, it is surprising that people don't yet appreciate the importance of learning how to work internationally— we promise you it is different from working with people in and from the United States. The earlier you learn and start practicing these skills (see, for example, *Success for the New Global Manager*), the better you will get and the more easily you will be able to work internationally when you finally need to.

Do different generations want to learn different things?

If we look at respondents' top ten developmental areas by generation (Table 9.2), we see that five developmental areas have made it onto every generation's list:

1. Leadership
2. Skills training in my field of expertise
3. Problem solving and decision making
4. Team building
5. Communication skills

These results indicate that there is broad agreement on areas that everyone is interested in developing—regardless of generation.

We do want to make a few comments on interesting differences and to note some specifics. Silents and Early Boomers put computer training in their top ten, whereas younger people did not. A reasonable explanation for this is that younger people (typically) started using computers when they were just out of elementary school. We asked people when they started using computers for tasks or work (not just to play video games) and found an unsurprising result, illustrated in Figure 9.1.

One result of the older generations' later start is that many Silents and Early Boomers feel less comfortable with computers than younger people do and would like to move further along the learning curve. Access to additional computer training, especially training that can be done on their own time on their own computer rather than in a public classroom setting, would clearly be useful to them.

Late Xers put public speaking and presentation skills, time management, and career planning in their top ten, whereas other generations did not. Younger people are primarily concerned with understanding how to do their work well and figuring out where they want to go and how to get there. Public speaking and presentation skills and time management skills are (sadly) not likely to have been learned in college. Younger people realize that they are likely to be deficient in these skills and want to learn them as quickly and efficiently as possible. Younger people are also concerned with figuring out where they want to go with their careers. The inclusion of career planning in their top ten suggests that some sort of course and/or coaching that helps them think through their career trajectory is something they desire.

Table 9.2. Top Ten Developmental Areas, by Generation.

Silents	Early Boomers	Late Boomers	Early Xers	Late Xers
Skills training in my field of expertise	Skills training in my field of expertise	Leadership	Leadership	Leadership
Computer training	Leadership	Skills training in my field of expertise	Skills training in my field of expertise	Problem solving, decision making
Team building	Computer training	Team building	Team building	Skills training in my field of expertise
Problem solving, decision making	Team building	Problem solving, decision making	Problem solving, decision making	Communication skills
Leadership	Problem solving, decision making	Strategic planning	Strategic planning	Self-awareness
Managing change	Managing change	Vision	Management and business skills	Team building
Diversity	Strategic planning	Managing change	Vision	Creativity
Communication skills	Vision	Communication skills	Communication skills	Public speaking and presentation skills
Self-awareness	Conflict management	Management and business skills	Self-awareness	Time management
Strategic planning	Communication skills	Conflict management	Managing change	Career planning

Figure 9.1.   Average Age of Beginning Computer Use.

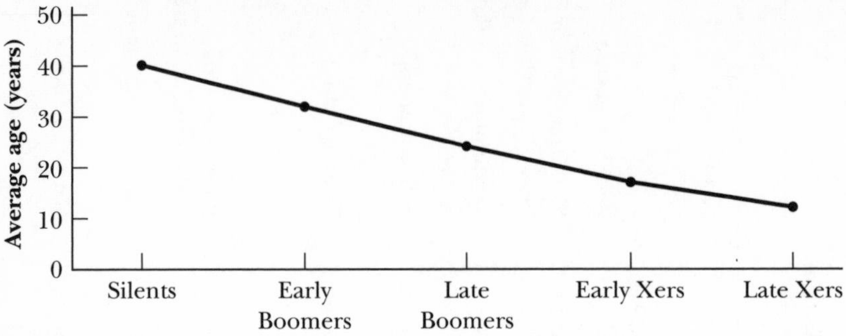

Most of the development priorities for Early Boomers, Late Boomers, and Early Xers are the same. People from these generations focus on development in the areas of strategic planning, managing change, and vision. They also included management, business skills, and conflict management in their top ten. It is interesting to note how similar the responses are from people of these generations. Why might this be? Why don't people of different generations want different types of development? Maybe generation is much less important than another factor in determining what development people want? (If you've read earlier chapters, perhaps you can guess what that factor is.)

Does organizational level influence what people want to learn more than their generation does?

A clear picture appears when you look at what people want to learn in terms of their organizational level rather than their generation. We've seen that some choices are influenced by people's generation (or, more likely, their age and length of time in the workforce), but most are areas of learning that people think they need to know to do their work well.

It is interesting that skills training and leadership shift in importance across the levels in the organization. For example, people in the top and executive ranks put leadership, strategic planning, team building, managing change, and vision in their top five, in contrast to people at other levels (see Table 9.3). This is

Table 9.3. Top Ten Developmental Areas, by Organizational Level.

Top and Executive	Upper Management	Management	Professional	First Level
Leadership	Leadership	Leadership	Skills training in my field of expertise	Skills training in my field of expertise
Strategic planning	Team building	Skills training in my field of expertise	Leadership	Computer training
Team building	Skills training in my field of expertise	Team building	Problem solving, decision making	Problem solving, decision making
Managing change	Strategic planning	Problem solving, decision making	Computer training	Communication skills
Vision	Vision	Strategic planning	Team building	Leadership
Skills training in my field of expertise	Managing change	Managing change	Communication skills	Team building
Problem solving, decision making	Problem solving, decision making	Vision	Self-awareness	Self-awareness
Communication skills	Management and business skills	Management and business skills	Conflict management	Conflict management
Management and business skills	Conflict management	Conflict management	Managing change	Creativity
Quality and process improvement	Self-awareness	Performance appraisal	Public speaking and presentation skills	Career planning

true for people in the top and executive ranks regardless of generation. Given the work required of executives, which tends to focus more on setting the direction and the vision of the organization than on actually producing widgets, it makes sense that these developmental areas would be at the top of their list.

Overall, leadership is at the top of the list in the management ranks; it declines in importance for professionals and then drops even further for people in the first level (the level below professionals). Skills training does the opposite: it is at the top for first-level employees and professionals, and drops in importance as we look from management to upper management to the top and executive levels. Problem solving and decision making are more important for people lower in the organization; team building becomes more important as people move up the organizational ladder.

As people move up, what we see is a transition from a need to develop more concrete skills (for example, computer training) at the lower levels to a need to develop those "soft skills" (leadership, strategic planning, vision, and the like) that are less concrete but more necessary at higher levels in the organization. Looking closely at Table 9.3, you can see a clear developmental plan for moving people from one level to another within the organization. The table lists what people at each level think they need to know and how important they think those skills are. Remember, these aren't things that "experts" are telling them they need to know; they are what the people themselves in the job are telling us (which makes the training an easier sell for those who have difficulty getting people to go to training).

For example, if you want to move someone from a professional position to a management position, you look at the development she needs for her current position (in the professional column) and the development necessary for the new position (the management column). You should think about how to add to the development she is receiving currently as a professional. (If you are laughing at this point because you and your people don't get any development, you will probably want to start by establishing a development plan.) For her to be most effective when you move her from the professional to management ranks, you will want to think about how she will get development in strategic planning, managing change, vision, management and business skills, conflict management, and performance appraisal. If you know the person is going to be moving into management in the next year or so, you can start helping her get the necessary development on the job or through other means right now, so that she can have a smooth transition into the new job and not feel quite as much as though she is in danger of drowning when she starts.

People moving from management to upper management or from upper management to executive positions often struggle with the increased scope of their new job. The leap from being a professional to managing a small team might be large, but the jump from a management position to a more strategic upper management or executive one is gigantic. Rather than focusing solely on getting something done, people at this level also need to focus on larger strategic, vision, and political issues. If an employee has spent her working life focused only on productivity and not on strategy or long-term vision, the shift can be difficult. Getting development in vision, strategic planning, communication skills, and quality and process improvement will be helpful in smoothing her transition into the new position.

How People Want to Learn

One trend we've observed is that organizations these days are altering their training to be computer based rather than relying on face-to-face training. The explanation we hear given for the change is that "that's how the younger people want their training—on the computer and whenever they want it, rather than during a class." This trend concerned us because although no one can deny that most people would prefer to have training come exactly when they want it without having to alter their schedules at all (what a nice life that would be!), the claim about generational learning preferences didn't jibe with what employees were telling us. So we spoke with dozens of people in organizations and compiled a list of 15 different methods that were used for learning—4 of which were computer based. Then we added a section into the questionnaire that focused on how people wanted to learn different types of information, and allowed people to choose up to 5 of the 15 options.

Another aspect of learning that we took into account is that not all skills are learned equally well the same way. For example, do you think you would learn how to use spreadsheets as well by discussing them in a group as you would by using a book or doing classroom work? Similarly, do you think you would learn as much about using political influence effectively by reading about it as you would by being coached or by practicing with peers? Obviously not. Different types of information are often learned better through different methods. We therefore asked people to tell us separately how they wanted to learn soft (people) skills and how they wanted to learn hard (technical) skills.

Education is the best provision for old age.
—ARISTOTLE (384–322 B.C.)

Participants had definite ideas about how they wanted to learn and about which methods they would prefer for soft and hard skills training. (Figure 9.2 shows the 15 learning methods respondents could choose from and the percentages of people who chose the particular methods.)

For learning soft skills, the top five methods chosen were

1. On-the-job training
2. One-on-one coaching
3. Peer interaction and feedback
4. Discussion groups
5. Live classroom instruction

These are all good ways to learn soft skills because they allow for feedback and for discussion and practice with other people, which are obviously critical for learning such skills as influence and conflict management.

For learning hard skills, the five most preferred methods were

1. On-the-job training
2. Workbooks and manuals
3. Books and reading
4. One-on-one coaching
5. Live classroom instruction

Hard skills do not typically require the person-to-person practice that soft skills often do, and are therefore good candidates for

Figure 9.2. How Respondents Said They Wanted to Learn.

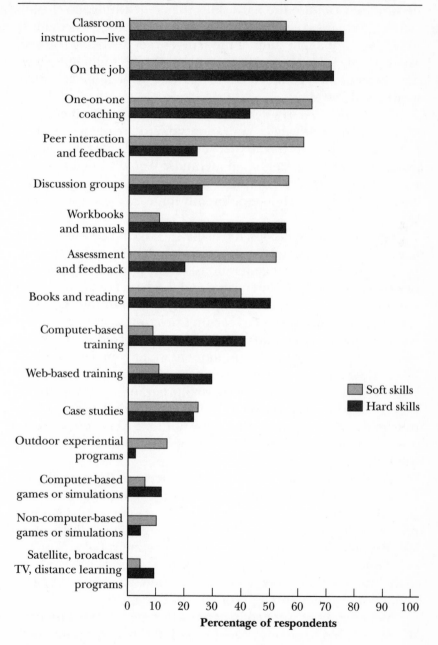

learning from a book or on a computer. Because people want to be sure they can use the hard skills they're learning, on-the-job training for hard skills is also a good choice because it encourages direct practical application of the skills as they are being learned. Many people learn through doing, so on-the-job training is an especially important complement to learning through more passive methods like reading.

So how do these results relate to the claims that younger people are the ones driving organizations toward greater use of computers in training? Is it true that younger people always prefer to learn through computer-based methods? Would younger people routinely choose the computer-based option when given the chance? Would they choose differently for learning soft skills than for hard skills?

With regard to soft skills, the major message is that there aren't many differences among the generations in how they want to learn (see Figure 9.3). For all generations, on-the-job training, one-on-one coaching, and peer interaction and feedback are the preferred methods for learning soft skills. Web-based training; satellite, broadcast TV, and distance learning programs; and computer-based games or simulations were the least preferred methods. Interestingly, the younger the respondent was, the more interested he or she was in outdoor experiential programs for learning soft skills. (Neither outdoor experiential programs nor case studies were among the most preferred learning methods, however.) Contrary to the stereotypes, neither Early nor Late Xers were more interested than Silents, Early Boomers, or Late Boomers in learning soft skills via a computer.

There were a few more differences between the generations when it comes to learning hard (technical) skills (see Figure 9.4). Early Boomers, Late Boomers, and Early Xers were more interested than were Silents and Late Xers in learning these skills through Web-based training. These results directly contradict the widespread belief that the youngest group would be most likely to want to learn in this way. Late Xers were no more interested than were other generations in learning through computer-based media.

All generations were consistently interested in learning hard skills through one-on-one coaching and workbooks and manuals. All generations were also interested in learning hard skills through

Figure 9.3. How Respondents Said They Wanted to Learn Soft Skills, by Generation.

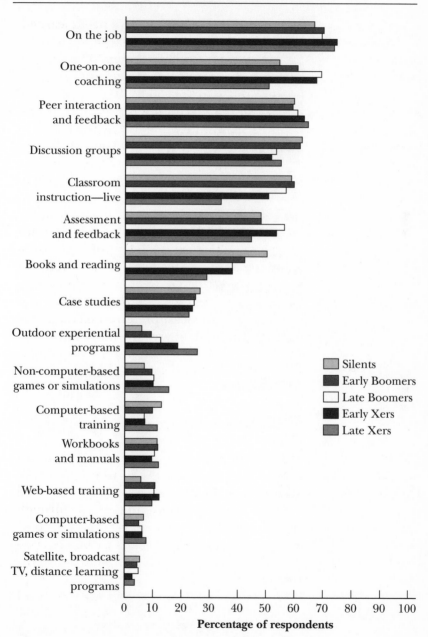

**Figure 9.4. How Respondents Said They Wanted
to Learn Hard Skills, by Generation.**

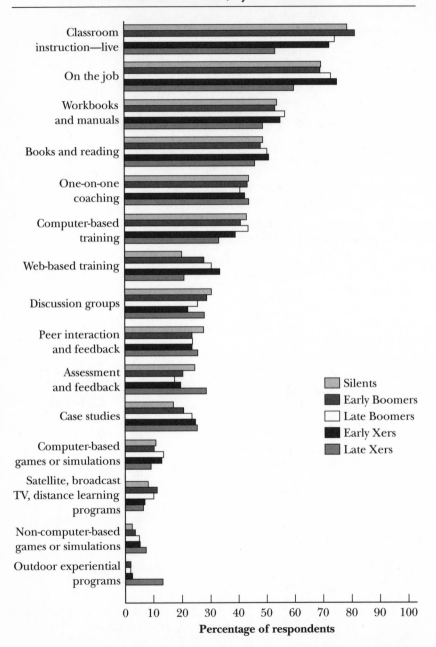

on-the-job training and live classroom work, though Late Xers were less in favor of classroom work than were the other generations. Overall, Late Xers were significantly less interested than were all other generations in learning hard skills (or soft skills, for that matter) through classroom instruction. Perhaps this is because Late Xers are more likely than the other generations to be currently enrolled in educational courses outside the workplace and are already spending a lot of time in classrooms.

Everyone Wants to Learn

It should be clear by this point that everyone wants to learn, wants to learn a variety of new skills, and wants to learn in about the same ways. People of all generations want to make sure they have the training necessary to do their current job well. They are also interested in what they need to be learning to get to the next level in their organization.

People of all generations said they understood that they need to learn, and they were concerned about how they were going to get access to the learning they need. Many respondents talked about how much they want development and how difficult it is to get the development they want because of lack of time and resources. Respondents talked about how they often felt they had to make a choice between development and spending time with their families. They said that often their employer wouldn't allow them to do the necessary learning and development during work time, despite the fact that the employer was going to directly benefit from their development. Under those circumstances, many people put development in the "nice to have, but not as high a priority as my family" category, and said they wouldn't end up doing it now even though they felt they needed it.

Unfortunately, the organizational reality of learning and development is that there are not unlimited resources to meet people's needs. Organizations seldom put aside the amount of money necessary to do training properly, and almost never put aside the amount of time people will need to learn everything they should know to do their best at the job. Meeting the learning and development needs of all employees just isn't going to happen, and as long as everyone understands that up front, everyone will be less frustrated. The good news is that our results show what development people want and how they want it. Using these results (see Tables 9.2 and 9.3) can help reduce everyone's frustration level by showing where (and how) efforts and resources can effectively be directed.

How This Applies to You

If you are a manager, coach, or HR professional, think about (1) what your people actually need to know before they start a job, (2) what they need to learn while they're in a job, and (3) how you can help them get the needed learning and development. Given the likely restrictions in your budget of both money and time that you can put toward development, it is beyond wonderful that most people of all generations want to learn on the job. So what you need to do is figure out how to do it!

If you look at Table 9.3, you can see some of the major areas of development people think they need to do particular jobs. If you take that as a starting point, you can assess an individual's strengths, weaknesses, and specific developmental needs in relation to the position she is going to be going into or that you are trying to develop her for. Once you understand what she has, doesn't have, and needs, you can go about deciding how that particular individual's development should occur. Development targeted at an individual's needs is more effective than wasting time and resources by making everyone go through cookie-cutter training that doesn't necessarily meet his or her learning needs. If the person needs development in soft skills, you should probably opt for on-the-job training combined with one-on-one coaching and peer interaction and feedback. You might also think about some sort of classroom instruction to jump-start and focus the process (especially for Silents, Early Boomers, Late Boomers, and Early Xers). Even if you can't make sure everyone has all the development she needs, you can definitely make sure she has the most important information and that she is receiving the development in the most useful and transferable way.

> Give me a young man in whom there is something of the old, and an old man with something of the young; guided so, a man may grow old in body, but never in mind.
> —Cicero (Marcus Tullius Cicero, 106–43 b.c.)

Another critical aspect of development is follow-up—ensuring that the person has actually learned what he was supposed to learn. Just because someone has gone through an experience does not mean he has learned from that experience, because not everyone is equally proficient at processing what he is going through in such a way as to actually learn from his experience. This is part of the reason that a structured learning plan, with specific check-ins by you or a coach, is critical in making sure that people actually learn from what they experience.

If at this point you're feeling lost, mildly frustrated, and as if you're hanging out on a limb because you know that this is a good idea but have no one in your organization to help you figure it out, we promise it isn't terribly difficult. If you're good with follow-through you can definitely put together a learning plan—a lot of it is about consistency and planning. We're not going to go through all of the details here, but there are *many* books that will help you, and some of the ones we think are best are listed in the References and Suggested Reading section at the back of this book.

If you are an individual employee, you might want to count on your organization, your boss, or your HR department to take care of structuring your learning. (Get real!) Unfortunately that isn't as likely to happen as you might hope. More important, what you learn and how you learn it have more effect on you than they do on everyone else. So if you want development, you have to make it happen. The fact is, although the organization may lose a bit if you don't know as much as you should for a position, *you* are really the one who is going to lose out, because you aren't going to do as well as you could, which will probably result in poorer evaluations, which of course results in fewer opportunities for promotion (and probably lower pay), which renders the long-term trajectory of your career not as pleasant as perhaps you would like.

> [When asked late in his life why he was studying geometry]
> If I should not be learning now, when should I be?
> —Attributed by Lacydes to Diogenes (c. 241 b.c.)

Understanding that it is ultimately up to you, you need to think about what you need to learn to do well in your current job, what you need to learn for your next (potential) job, and what is useful to learn that may not necessarily be immediately applicable but will make you more marketable in the long term.

This all may sound overwhelming, or it may not.

We know you already have a full-time job and too much to do.

We know you have a family and friends you would like to see occasionally.

Now it probably does sound overwhelming!

You have to decide what your priorities are. People generally work to develop themselves because they like to learn and because they think that their work opportunities are going to be better in the long run if they improve their skills and increase their knowledge. And before you ask, no, there are no guarantees. You may go to the trouble of learning something that doesn't have an immediate payoff, but that doesn't mean that in the long run it wasn't worth learning. So when you are thinking about what development you need, be sure to consult with people in your organization whom you respect and who you think know where you could possibly be going with your career. And if you can manage to find a boss or more senior person who is willing to coach you and really think about what is best for you and your career (not just what is best for him or the organization), count yourself lucky, appreciate the gift he is giving you, and plan to do the same for someone else in the future.

Better, Cheaper, Faster—Choose Two

Many people think that computer-based learning is the best thing to come along in years: it can be spread widely (thus theoretically making it cheaper per person); it can be done in between other things so that people can fit it in quickly (thus making it faster); and people can go at their own pace and review over and over (or skip) areas where they need more (or less) information (thus making it better).

You've probably heard the saying, "Better, cheaper, faster—choose two." It applies all too well to computer-based training (CBT), which people often think is the be-all and end-all—the ultimate learning method.

Yes, in some cases CBT is cheaper and faster, but are people actually learning as much through this method (which wouldn't make it as good, let alone "better")?

Yes, CBT can be very well designed to aid learning (better), and can be very fast, but if it is a high-end product, will it really be cheaper in the end?

And if it is better and cheaper . . . how quickly are you likely to get a product when you want it to be very good and want to pay a cut rate for it? CBT isn't likely to be faster if it is both good and cheap.

Don't misunderstand us, we think CBT is wonderful for some topics; we just don't think it is the silver bullet for all training and learning. Remember, it hasn't been that long since people were touting television as the ultimate learning tool! So if you are really going to try to use wide-scale CBT, you should probably think about a few things before you implement it.

How Will You Be Sure That Your People Actually Pay Attention During the Training?

We talked with a doctor friend who was doing computer-based continuing education coursework because he couldn't attend the class in person. What he did was to put the CD in his computer and come back periodically to hit Enter in the appropriate places. He was seeing patients at the time and was *not* paying any attention to the training he was supposed to be getting.

How are you going to prevent this sort of behavior? Do you want to try to prevent it? In this case, he had to take an exam on the subject later, so he figured he'd learn the material using a textbook before the exam rather than sit through a terminally boring (so to speak) CD-based learning course.

If you are providing CBT that you expect people to remember afterwards, making them take (and pass) an exam on the material is a good idea. Otherwise, how do you know they actually learned what they were supposed to have learned? Do you trust them to sit down and pay complete attention when they have 1,001 other things they have to do or would prefer to be doing?

At this point someone is going to be thinking, "But we're all adults, and we should trust people to do the right thing and pay attention and go through the coursework online. I'm sure they will if we thoroughly explain why it is so important."

Right. Sure. Uh huh.

The reality is that people are busy and they have to make choices about how they are going to spend their scarce resources (in this case, time). They will give priority to what *must* be done over what would be nice to get done. People are unlikely to pay much attention to CBT that takes place online or during unsupervised or personal time and that does not require a test afterwards. They may have the best of intentions, but people are likely to categorize information they are not going to be held responsible for as "nice to know" rather than "have to know or I will be punished."

What Are You Going to Use the CBT For?

If you're teaching chemistry or accounting or math (anything that has problem sets that can be done using numbers) or providing content that needs to be memorized, CBT might be a good choice. It is apparent from the responses that people from the generations older than the Late Xers are predisposed to liking CBT for this kind of information.

However, if you're thinking about using CBT as a stand-alone for teaching soft skills, you need to think about it again . . . and again . . . and again—until you change your mind! The results of our study clearly indicate that people do not want to learn soft skills through computer-based methods or through books, probably because they know it is pretty much a waste of time. You can certainly give people information through these methods, but without live practice, they aren't likely to learn people skills. If you want to teach someone how to identify resistance to a concept in a person's facial expressions and body position and then how to influence the person to take a different perspective, computers and books are probably not the best tools for the job.

Who Will Participate in the CBT?

We know that older people want more training in the use of computers, especially if they can do it privately, so they are probably a good audience. We know that Late Xers are less interested than older groups in CBT. Probably the best option is to use CBT as a supplement to other types of training (on-the-job, coaching, and the like). In this way, people can get the information they need at their own pace and on their own time, while also having a chance to practice what they've learned with others (and therefore being held publicly accountable for the material they are supposed to know). There are a number of very successful development programs that use this combination of methods, and the reports about them are that people appreciate the combination more than they do either of the methods by themselves.

What You Should Have Learned from This Chapter

- Of employees surveyed, 97% said that it was important for them to learn on the job, and 90% said they *were* learning on the job.
- What people want to learn is related to what they need for their job, not to their generation.
- Younger people do not want to learn everything via a computer.
- Older people want to learn some things via a computer.
- Everyone wants to learn on the job.
- Everyone thinks coaching is a good idea.
- People are savvy about what they need to learn, what they want to learn, and how they want to learn. Listen to them.

Almost Everyone Wants a Coach

We've heard more times than we can count that younger people are constantly asking for feedback and can't get enough of it—in other words, they're needy. We've also heard that older people don't want any feedback at all—they almost always take offense at it. But according to our research, everyone wants to know how he or she is doing and wants to learn how to do better. Different generations have had different experiences giving and receiving feedback—and those experiences have shaped the views they express regarding feedback. Put simply, feedback can come in many forms, and our research suggests that people of all generations would like to receive it from a coach.

Consider what this young executive (Victoria) had to say about how she approaches giving feedback to her direct reports:

> Every couple of months we sit down and look over what they're doing. We talk about what job they want next, what they're learning, and what they need to learn to get where they want to go. Over lunch we think through what is going on, and brainstorm about what they need to be doing more of, and what they might need to do differently. We concentrate on creating a list of actionable items that they can do in the short term, and set up a check-in meeting to make sure that the plans are working out as expected. It seems to me that my people improve more quickly, make fewer errors, and feel better about themselves, their jobs, and me as their boss when we do this. It takes a bit of time, but doing this type of on-going coaching really pays off for everyone in the long run. It works much better than the traditional once or twice a year check-ins! No more uncomfortable surprises when it comes to review time, because

they know what they have and haven't succeeded in, even before I do! Even better, they become more proactive in suggesting their own performance improvement plans because they know where I stand on what they're doing, and they know that I can be counted on to help them along the way.

Wouldn't you love to have a boss like this!

Coaching for development has become more common in organizations in the past few years.

Coaching is first and foremost a way to facilitate learning. For leaders and managers at all levels and in all kinds of organizations, the most powerful lessons arise from experience. But it's not enough just to have the experience. People need a way to process that experience—to reflect on it, to place it in context, and to create plans for acting on what they have learned. Coaching is an effective tool that can be used to help people learn from their experience [Ting and Scisco, 2006, pp. 10–11].

Coaching is versatile, efficient, and targeted, and it provides the personal support and looking-over-the-shoulder reminders that help learners apply what they are learning. Coaching is a wonderful strategy for encouraging development because it gives learners someone to whom they are responsible and of whom they can ask questions. Even if people aren't having particular problems at work that are hampering their development, their having someone to help them think through how they could handle situations differently or understand what types of information and learning might be useful. It is also a great way to help people continue to learn and improve while on the job. And in a world where there is less and less time for training that takes employees out of the workplace, constant improvement while on the job is the dream scenario of every employer.

Research

Many people have asked us whether all employees want coaching or whether it is just a fad for younger people. So we asked people of all generations the following questions:

Do you think that coaching is useful for your development?

Whom do you want as a coach?

How do you want to interact with your coach?

How often do you want to interact with your coach?

What do you want the focus of the coaching relationship to be?

Do you have the skills to coach someone in your organization?

Do people think that coaching is useful for their development?

As we discussed in the chapter on learning (Principle 9), one-on-one coaching was one of the most frequently chosen developmental options for learning both soft and hard skills. There were no generational differences related to wanting one-on-one coaching, and more than 85% of respondents of all generations and at all organizational levels thought that coaching either was or would be useful for their own development (see Figure 10.1).

Whom do people want as a coach?

It isn't always clear who should be doing the coaching, so we asked respondents to tell us whom they wanted as a coach (see Figure 10.2). Silents, Early Boomers, Late Boomers, and Early Xers said they want a senior colleague, an expert in the field, or someone

Figure 10.1. Percentage of Respondents Who Said That Coaching Is Useful for Development, by Generation and by Organizational Level.

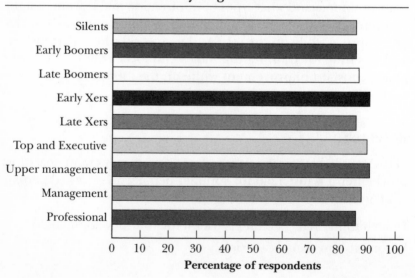

Percentage of respondents

Figure 10.2. Coach Preference, by Generation.

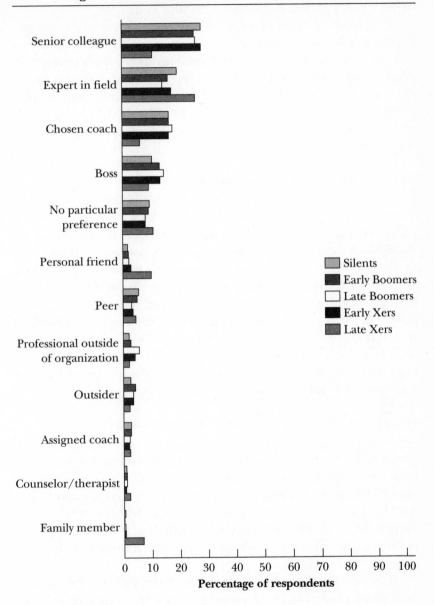

they have chosen themselves. Late Xers said they want an expert in the field, a personal friend, or a senior colleague.

A different pattern emerged when we looked at whom people at different levels in organizations want as a coach. As shown in Figure 10.3, people of all organizational levels prefer a senior colleague above everyone else. A second choice was an expert in the field as a coach, which was more desirable to professionals than it was to people in management. Generally, the boss or a coach chosen by the individual is more desirable to people higher in the organization.

How do people want to interact with their coach?

Everyone, regardless of generation or level in the organization, overwhelmingly chose face-to-face coaching (see Figures 10.4 and 10.5). No one preferred the telephone or e-mail for coaching. Although younger people and people in the professional and first levels of an organization said they wouldn't mind being coached by e-mail, they really would prefer working face-to-face. With regard to coaching by telephone, it is interesting to note that more people in the top and executive ranks said they prefer that method than did anyone else (but still not much). This was probably a result of their crazy schedules and the difficulty of consistently keeping coaching appointments—in other words, if they really want coaching, they have to take it any way they can get it.

How often do people want to interact with their coach?

Generally, people said they want to interact with their coaches weekly to monthly (see Figure 10.6). Overall, younger generations preferred more frequent coaching interaction than older generations did. Late Xers preferred every week. Early Xers also preferred weekly interaction, though almost equal numbers found twice a month or monthly acceptable as well. Late Boomers, Early Boomers, and Silents were about equally split among weekly, twice a month, and monthly.

Similarly, people at all organizational levels want to interact with their coaches weekly, twice a month, or monthly; people at lower levels desired more frequent contact than did people at higher levels (see Figure 10.7).

Figure 10.3. Coach Preference, by Organizational Level.

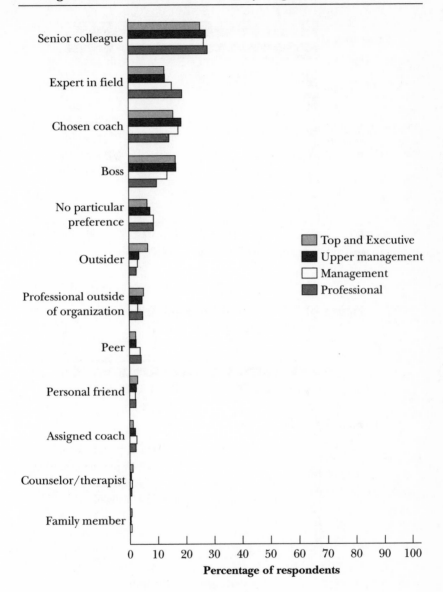

Figure 10.4. Preferred Coaching Interaction, by Generation.

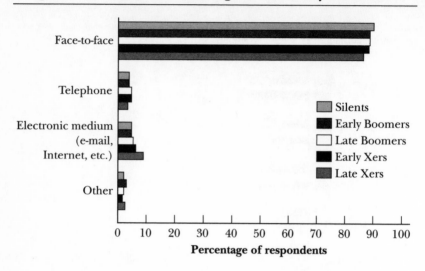

Figure 10.5. Preferred Coaching Interaction, by Organizational Level.

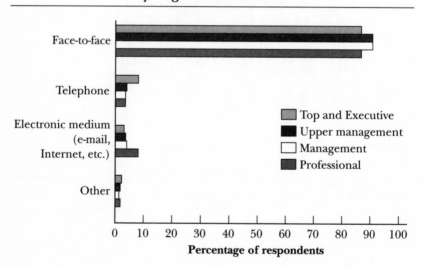

Figure 10.6. Preferred Coaching Frequency, by Generation.

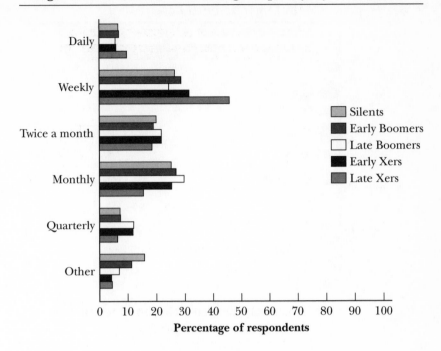

Percentage of respondents

What should be the focus of the coaching relationship?

Overall, people wanted coaching to focus on their job, their career, or leadership development. However, there were differences in how the generations wanted to focus the coaching (see Figure 10.8). Late Xers wanted the coaching to focus mostly on life and their career and were less interested in focusing on their current job or on leadership development. Early Xers and Late Boomers would like the focus to be on their career and on leadership development. Early Boomers and Silents were also interested in focusing on their career and on leadership development, but many of them would be happy with the coaching focusing on their particular job.

When we looked at the responses by organizational level, a different picture appeared (see Figure 10.9). People in the professional ranks also wanted the focus to be on their careers, with a

Figure 10.7. Preferred Coaching Frequency, by Organizational Level.

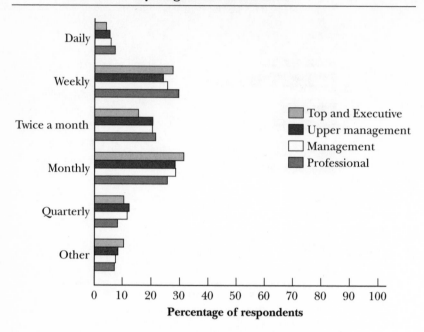

Figure 10.8. Preferred Coaching Focus, by Generation.

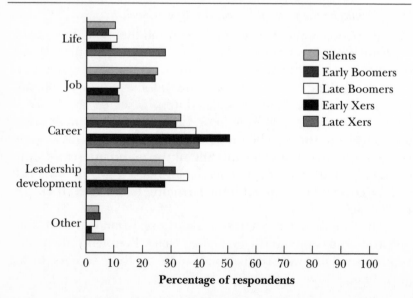

**Figure 10.9. Preferred Coaching Focus,
by Organizational Level.**

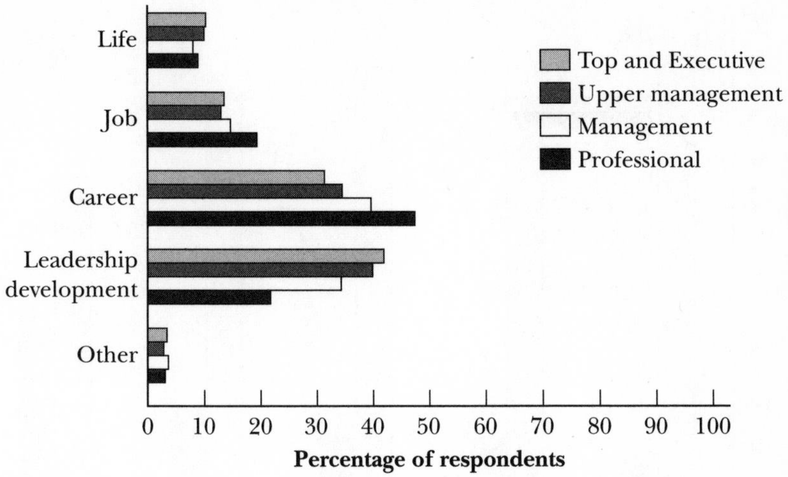

secondary focus on the particular job and on leadership development. The picture shifted slightly when we looked to management,
upper management, and the top and executive levels. Although
people at all levels were interested in coaching focused on both
their career and leadership development, the interest in focusing
on leadership increased with each step higher in the organization.

Do people think they have the skills to coach someone in their organization?

Most people of all generations thought that they have the skills to
coach someone in their own organization, although the percentage of people who said this increased with age (see Figure 10.10).
Late Xers were the least likely to say they have the skills to be a
coach—very reasonable, since they're the youngest group with
(presumably) the least experience.

Similarly, people at all levels in organizations said that they
have the skills to be a coach (see Figure 10.11). Professionals were
the least likely to say this.

We also asked people to tell us what skills they would like to ac-
quire (or improve) if they were going to be coaches. They said they
would need

**Figure 10.10. Responses to the Question, "Do You Have
the Skills to Coach Someone?" by Generation.**

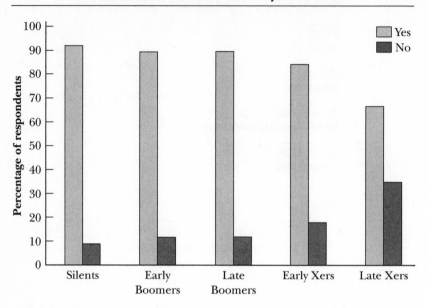

- More knowledge
- Greater experience
- Better political acumen
- Better communication skills
- Training on how to be a coach

Many people also said they had the skills to coach, but not the
time. They said they would be happy to act as coaches if their organizations decided coaching was important enough to put time—
and therefore money—toward it.

> Would need to work on patience and listening.
> —Silent

> I have difficulty confronting persons with their negative behaviors. I "velvet
> glove" it so much that they do not always recognize their need to change.
> I am not good at organization—to mentor or coach someone effectively, I
> would possibly need to "track" behavior or performance. I note those things
> mentally in supervision, but do not consistently keep track of the details.
> —Early Boomer

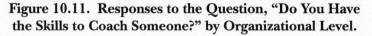

Figure 10.11. Responses to the Question, "Do You Have the Skills to Coach Someone?" by Organizational Level.

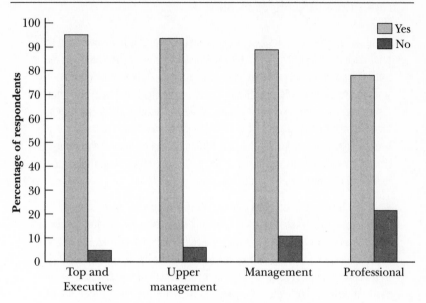

Have the skills, don't have the time. Mentoring/coaching
has taken a back seat in my organization.
—Late Boomer

I could improve on how to push them in the right
direction without doing it for them. I also need
improvement on handling difficult confrontations.
—Early Xer

[I would need another] few years on the
job in order to be taken seriously.
—Late Xer

Almost Everyone Wants a Coach

The research clearly demonstrates that almost everyone—regardless of generation or level in the organization—wants a coach.
Similarly, almost everyone thinks that she has the skills to be a
coach—or that she could learn them given organizational support.

Even when they teach, men learn.
—SENECA THE YOUNGER (4 B.C.–65 A.D.), *Epistulae*

How This Applies to You

Consider the following example.

> Craig is a director-level, Ivy League–educated M.D. and M.B.A. working in the pharmaceutical industry. Though he has had an unusually productive career until this point, he believes that a key element that has been missing from his work in organizations is a mentor or career coach who could help him gain more from his learning experiences and strategize about what would be best for his career in the future. He feels so strongly about it that it is one of the reasons he is leaving his current position. Although Craig asked for coaching, his boss in the organization feels that it isn't part of his job to coach Craig and is unwilling to hire a coach for him.
>
> This turns out to be a bad move on the boss's part, because Craig is now leaving for a rival pharmaceutical company where his new boss has indicated that it is a priority for him to develop and coach the medical directors in the firm. Craig knows he can learn more and faster if he has a coach to assist him in his development. He also knows that the more he learns and improves, the more value he will bring to his organization. In this industry (as in many others), the organization's future wealth comes from the intellectual capital of the employees. Craig understands that and is grateful that the new boss will take an interest in his development.

Clearly, Craig had several options. And lack of a coach was probably not the only thing motivating him to move on. But if you consider the other principles we've explored, you can probably see where *desire for a coach* could act as a statement representative of all sorts of employee issues: the need to learn, the need to feel valued, the need to feel that one is making a valued contribution, and the need to ensure that one's position holds some clout.

If you seek a coach at work and are finding that no one in management is supportive, then it may be time to ask the other, seemingly tougher, questions:

- Can I get the development I need without a coach?
- What is my future here?
- Do I feel valued? If not, why not?
- Do I feel that I am adding value? Can I add greater value next year than this year?

- Is the organization invested in my development? If so, why don't I have a coach?
- Does the organization (read: my manager) need to be educated in this regard? Is this something I can contribute to, or is it too much to handle, given my priorities and where I am in my career?

If you have a coach at work or can at least identify someone who could serve as your coach, then bear in mind that the coach may not be sure what to offer and when. You may need to guide your own development process as much as the coach does.

Also keep in mind that in many organizations, coaches are not formally designated. Coaching may or may not be incorporated into a manager's performance goals or measured as part of his or her review. If your organization has no formal coaching methodology or expectations, think "mentor" instead. Try to find a more experienced person in whom you can place your trust, and seek counsel from him or her. Sometimes the most effective coach you can have doesn't even work within the company.

If you are interested in learning more about how to be a coach, we recommend you take a look at *The CCL Handbook of Coaching* (Ting and Scisco, 2006). A list of additional reading can be found in the References and Suggested Reading section at the end of this book.

If You Are a Manager

If you can set up coaching relationships for your people, do it. Coaching is one of the most versatile, efficient, and targeted methods for learning that exists. It also provides the personal support that learners need to make sure they actually apply what they are learning (something that is often an issue in other learning methods).

You don't have to go outside and pay for coaching; much of the time you can set up a coaching program using your own people. Most of the survey respondents said they could act as coaches—and that they were willing to coach if their organizations would set aside some of their work time for it (instead of just adding it as one more task). Many said they would be happy to get the additional training they need to be a good coach.

If you are going to set up a coaching program or coaching relationship, it is obviously best to begin by talking with the coach and coachee about their expectations for the coaching. This chapter can give you a few ideas about where to start and what to expect. People at all levels in organizations and of all generations want basically the same thing when it comes to their coaching. Virtually all employees prefer weekly to monthly face-to-face coaching that is focused on their job, their career, or leadership development (or a combination of these). And they want coaching from a senior colleague, an expert in the field, their boss, or someone they choose themselves.

Think back to what the young executive said at the beginning of this chapter. This woman is an example of a boss acting as a coach for her own people. Coaching is a wonderful strategy for a boss to use in encouraging people to constantly improve in their current position. But her story didn't end there.

> About a year later, Victoria was being evaluated (about her management and leadership style and effectiveness) and received feedback from her people that she wasn't giving them as much feedback "in the moment" as they wanted. They said she was very good at career planning, mentoring, giving positive reinforcement, and structuring work, but that they wanted to know more immediately when they'd done something wrong. Unfortunately it wasn't clear from the format of the feedback instrument whether they thought she wasn't doing what they wanted at all or if they just wanted her to tell them more often when they screwed up.
>
> After looking at the feedback and discussing it with her own coach, Victoria decided that it was impossible to tell what was going on and that she was going to ask her people. Initially she thought she might ask them as a group, but she decided that she wouldn't get enough individual information that way. To avoid putting her people on the spot, she planned to bring this feedback up during the upcoming performance evaluation meetings. During those meetings she was going to mention the feedback she had received and was going to ask each direct report what she could do to better meet the direct report's needs. In other words, after coaching her direct report, she was going to ask the direct report for coaching. In that way she would both receive the information she needed to help her direct reports and help them practice coaching themselves. (Note: Victoria did as she had planned, and was told by her direct reports that she was giving them plenty of feedback—they just wanted her to

let them fail occasionally so they could learn from their own mistakes rather than showing them how they could be successful in the moment.)

In short, people of all generations and at all levels in organizations want coaching and think it would be useful for them to have in their current positions. If you can figure out a way to get coaching for yourself and your employees, do it, because it will provide real benefits to your employees and to your organization. You'll find that you benefit, too!

What You Should Have Learned from This Chapter

- People from every generation and at every level want a coach.
- You don't have to hire someone to coach your direct reports— you can be a coach.
- You can have your employees be coaches by providing them with more knowledge, greater experience, better communication skills, and specific training on how to be a coach.
- Coaching is one of the best methods for helping your employees learn and improve because the learning is more individualized and targeted than any class can be.
- If you are an employee who wants coaching, you should ask for it.

Conclusion

Not by age but by capacity is wisdom acquired.
TITUS MACCIUS PLAUTUS (254–184 B.C.)

The generation gap wasn't invented in the United States in the 1950s and 1960s; as far as we can tell, it has existed as long as there have been people. Some of the quotations we've used show that cross-generational animosity was an issue at least as far back as 400 B.C.

Because the generation gap is probably as old as humankind, we won't pretend to think that what we've said here is going to completely retire it. We have tried to point out where the gap isn't as large as people think it is (at least in the United States—we can't speak confidently yet about the generation gap in other parts of the world) and to show that conflicts at work arising from the generation gap are dwarfed by conflict that stems from other sources, chief among them the desire to maintain or increase clout. And *that* story too is as old as time.

There are always going to be conflicts. You're going to see younger and older people disagreeing, and these conflicts are often going to continue to look as though they are caused by generational differences. But at least now you know that such fundamental differences aren't really the cause of these problems; you know that the people involved probably want similar things.

Knowing this, when you see a conflict that others identify as being caused by the generation gap, you know that you need to look deeper for the real causes of the conflict. Understanding its real roots can help you decide what you can do to eliminate—or at least mitigate—it.

The next time you hear someone at work talking about a person from another generation in a negative way—whether older or younger—remember that what is being said isn't just about disliking that individual's clothes or hairstyle or earrings or way of speaking. Often underlying the specific complaints is the belief that the individual isn't doing things as he or she should—with the attendant assumption that the person complaining gets to decide how someone should behave. In some cases, the person who is so upset is seeking either to maintain or to increase his or her own clout by finding something wrong with someone else of another generation.

What You Need to Do

You have to accept generational conflict as an inevitable part of work and deal with it the way you do all the other status issues in the workplace. Remember that whenever you go into any conversation, the relative clout of the participants is part of the dynamic. Remember that issues surrounding who should be listening to whom, whose opinions should be listened to most closely, and who should be reporting to whom are often more about how much respect, deference, and control people think they should have than about actual competence or productivity at work.

People assume that with experience comes knowledge. That is true in theory, but we all know the old saying about someone who has had one year of experience—20 times. What is important about experience is the knowledge gained from it, and how much knowledge people accumulate from their experiences has nothing to do with age and everything to do with how good they are at learning from those experiences. True, older people have had more experiences and have had more time to process and accumulate knowledge than have younger people—but that doesn't mean that they've taken advantage of their head start.

Part of the human condition is the understanding that older people should be deferred to because of their greater experience and therefore (it is assumed) greater knowledge. The cultural norm that older people have more authority than younger ones is deeply ingrained, even as people talk about how "youth focused" the United States is. The assumption that older people have more authority isn't necessarily a bad thing; it just causes problems when younger people are promoted ahead of older ones, which turns the typical authority relationship upside down.

*"Take a load off, Leonard—we're watching
Generations X and Y duke it out."*

Luckily the generation gap at work is one more of appearance than of substance. As we said in the beginning,

- People want about the same things at work, no matter what generation they are from.
- You can effectively work with or manage people from all generations.

You just need to remember—and put into practice—the principles we've discussed here.

1. All generations have similar values.
2. Everyone wants respect.
3. Trust matters.
4. People want leaders who are credible and trustworthy.
5. Organizational politics is a problem—no matter how old (or young) you are.
6. No one really likes change.
7. Loyalty depends on the context, not on the generation.
8. It's as easy to retain a young person as an older one—if you do the right things.
9. Everyone wants to learn—more than just about anything else.
10. Almost everyone wants a coach.

You can use some of our suggestions—which are based on our data and experience—for applying these principles. And you'll undoubtedly come up with your own techniques that work in the context of your own workplace.

Remember, you don't have to tie yourself into knots (or worse!) trying to accommodate each generation's individual whims, and you don't have to worry about learning a new set of whims when the next generation comes along. People from different generations are largely alike in what they think, believe, and want from their work life. Once people accept this fact, and make their actions consistent with the principles that apply to working with people of all generations, the gap will be retired.

Answers to a Few Questions

There are a few questions people typically ask that aren't directly related to the ten principles discussed in this book, so we thought we'd put the answers here.

What about generational differences in other countries? Are they the same as the ones described in this book? We don't know. We are gathering data, and as soon as we have enough we will start doing analyses.

Because this book covers just the United States, are you going to do the same kind of book for other regions of the world? It depends on what we find and what we think the demand will be. So the answer right now is "maybe." If you think it is a good idea, let us know of your interest.

What's next? We're currently working on developing something we call the World Leadership Survey, which will ask about leadership all around the world. The questions will be asked of people in their native language (rather than just in English, as we did with the current study). Obviously this is a large undertaking. If you're interested in seeing where we are with it, please visit the Center for Creative Leadership's Web site at www.ccl.org and look for a link to the World Leadership Survey. We hope that by the time you read this it will be up and running, and you'll be able to participate!

Percentage of Respondents Who Placed Each Value in Their Top Ten, by Generation

VALUE	Silents (%)	Early Boomers (%)	Late Boomers (%)	Early Xers (%)	Late Xers (%)	Overall (%)
ACHIEVEMENT	35	45	53	50	33	48
ACTIVITY	3	5	5	8	6	6
ADVANCEMENT	10	19	24	28	29	24
ADVENTURE	4	12	11	15	9	12
AESTHETICS	9	7	3	3	4	4
AFFILIATION	10	5	3	4	9	5
AFFLUENCE	10	10	12	16	6	12
AUTHORITY	13	5	6	6	6	6
AUTONOMY	31	28	25	24	15	25
BALANCE	31	37	41	43	28	39
CHALLENGE	18	16	23	22	13	20
CHANGE/VARIETY	12	17	14	13	5	14
COLLABORATION	15	13	14	11	10	12
COMMUNITY	24	21	11	12	18	15
COMPETENCE	47	48	50	46	20	46
COMPETITION	1	1	3	5	1	3
COURAGE	28	27	21	22	26	24

VALUE	Silents (%)	Early Boomers (%)	Late Boomers (%)	Early Xers (%)	Late Xers (%)	Overall (%)
CREATIVITY	34	30	21	20	25	24
ECONOMIC SECURITY	34	31	31	27	29	30
ENJOYMENT	13	18	24	32	34	25
FAME	0	1	0	6	6	3
FAMILY	53	60	76	78	78	72
FRIENDSHIP	19	21	23	28	53	26
HAPPINESS	31	40	45	52	59	46
HELP OTHERS	34	33	23	21	46	27
HUMOR	18	24	26	28	33	26
INFLUENCE	22	21	20	18	13	19
INTEGRITY	69	70	72	60	39	65
JUSTICE	38	35	23	17	18	24
LOCATION	16	12	19	16	4	15
LOVE	40	44	47	49	73	48
LOYALTY	18	19	16	18	41	19
ORDER	13	3	4	5	3	4
PERSONAL DEVELOPMENT	22	20	24	28	29	25
RECOGNITION	22	18	22	18	16	19
REFLECTION	9	10	6	6	5	7
RESPONSIBILITY	41	36	39	37	41	38
SELF-RESPECT	59	48	41	43	58	45
SPIRITUALITY	34	30	30	25	31	29
WISDOM	60	57	45	36	34	45

Note: The difference between two generations' responses is statistically significant (note for the statistically minded: "statistically significant" here is at the 99% confidence level or $p < 0.01$) if the difference between the two percentages is greater than the number that follows for each pair:

S = Silents; EB = Early Boomers; LB = Late Boomers; EX = Early Xers; LX = Late Xers

S – EB > 18%	EB – LB > 10%	LB – EX > 9%	EX – LX > 15%
S – LB > 17%	EB – EX > 10%	LB – LX > 15%	
S – EX > 17%	EB – LX > 16%		
S – LX > 23%			

For example, let's look at the data for ACHIEVEMENT:

	S	EB	LB	EX	LX
ACHIEVEMENT	35	45	53	50	33

We see that significantly more Late Boomers than Late Xers chose this value (53% versus 33%, with the difference of 20% being more than the cut-off difference of 15%). However, the difference between Early Boomers and Silents (45% versus 35%, or a difference of 10%) is smaller than the cut-off difference of 18% and hence is not statistically significant.

$N = 1,285$ (68 Silents, 316 Early Boomers, 410 Late Boomers, 411 Early Xers, and 80 Late Xers)

Percentage of Respondents Who Placed Each Value in Their Top Three, by Generation

VALUE	Silents (%)	Early Boomers (%)	Late Boomers (%)	Early Xers (%)	Late Xers (%)	Overall (%)
ACHIEVEMENT	3	12	16	14	3	13
ACTIVITY	0	1	0	1	1	1
ADVANCEMENT	1	1	4	5	4	3
ADVENTURE	0	1	1	2	0	1
AESTHETICS	3	0	0	0	1	0
AFFILIATION	0	1	0	0	1	0
AFFLUENCE	1	3	3	4	0	3
AUTHORITY	7	0	2	0	0	1
AUTONOMY	3	4	4	5	5	4
BALANCE	9	11	11	13	3	11
CHALLENGE	1	4	5	3	0	4
CHANGE/VARIETY	1	3	1	2	1	2
COLLABORATION	1	1	2	0	1	1
COMMUNITY	4	3	2	2	4	2
COMPETENCE	4	14	9	7	1	9
COMPETITION	0	0	1	0	0	0

VALUE	Silents (%)	Early Boomers (%)	Late Boomers (%)	Early Xers (%)	Late Xers (%)	Overall (%)
COURAGE	4	5	2	3	1	3
CREATIVITY	7	6	4	3	1	4
ECONOMIC SECURITY	9	15	10	9	8	11
ENJOYMENT	3	1	2	5	0	3
FAME	0	0	0	0	0	0
FAMILY	46	45	64	67	73	60
FRIENDSHIP	1	6	5	8	25	7
HAPPINESS	9	13	18	20	25	17
HELP OTHERS	6	3	3	3	13	3
HUMOR	1	4	3	3	5	4
INFLUENCE	0	2	1	2	0	1
INTEGRITY	46	32	29	24	11	28
JUSTICE	15	6	2	2	1	4
LOCATION	4	3	4	3	0	3
LOVE	26	27	29	32	49	31
LOYALTY	3	3	3	3	6	3
ORDER	0	0	1	1	0	1
PERSONAL DEVELOPMENT	3	5	3	4	5	4
RECOGNITION	1	3	5	3	1	4
REFLECTION	1	0	1	0	0	1
RESPONSIBILITY	10	7	4	7	4	6
SELF-RESPECT	22	21	14	16	19	17
SPIRITUALITY	25	21	23	17	28	21
WISDOM	15	13	10	7	1	9

Note: The difference between two generations' responses is statistically significant (note for the statistically minded: "statistically significant" here is at the 99% confidence level or $p < 0.01$) if the difference between the two percentages is greater than the number that follows for each pair:

S = Silents; EB = Early Boomers; LB = Late Boomers; EX = Early Xers; LX = Late Xers

S – EB > 18%   EB – LB > 10%   LB – EX > 9%   EX – LX > 15%
S – LB > 17 %   EB – EX > 10 %   LB – LX > 15 %
S – EX > 17%   EB – LX > 16%
S – LX > 23%

For example, let's look at the data for LOVE:

	S	EB	LB	EX	LX
LOVE	26	27	29	32	49

We see that significantly more Late Xers than Silents chose this value (49% versus 26%, with the difference of 23% being exactly the cut-off difference of 23%). However, the difference between Early Xers and Silents (32% versus 26%, or a difference of 6%) is smaller than the cut-off difference of 17% and hence is not statistically significant.

N = 1,285 (68 Silents, 316 Early Boomers, 410 Late Boomers, 411 Early Xers, and 80 Late Xers)

Percentage of Respondents Who Placed Each Leadership Attribute in Their Top Ten, by Generation

LEADERSHIP ATTRIBUTE	Silents (%)	Early Boomers (%)	Late Boomers (%)	Early Xers (%)	Late Xers (%)	Overall (%)
A GOOD COACH	38	33	46	40	36	40
A GOOD TEACHER	29	28	27	32	30	29
ADVENTURESOME	15	16	9	15	14	13
BALANCED	18	25	25	28	25	26
CANDID AND HONEST	32	28	31	25	20	27
CREATIVE	32	33	22	26	33	28
CREDIBLE	65	74	75	71	48	69
CULTURALLY SENSITIVE LEADER	18	16	9	9	6	10
DEDICATED	38	32	33	33	63	38
DELEGATING	50	30	29	23	10	26
DEPENDABLE	41	38	49	46	66	48
DIPLOMATIC	18	31	26	26	10	24
DURABLE	9	19	15	22	20	18
ENCOURAGING	44	50	53	46	54	50

LEADERSHIP ATTRIBUTE	Silents (%)	Early Boomers (%)	Late Boomers (%)	Early Xers (%)	Late Xers (%)	Overall (%)
ENERGETIC	18	16	11	19	28	17
ENTERPRISING	9	14	12	13	8	12
EXPERIENCED	38	32	41	36	43	38
FARSIGHTED	53	57	59	54	29	52
FOCUSED	32	39	44	43	59	44
GLOBAL LEADERSHIP IMAGE	3	2	4	5	0	3
GLOBALLY INNOVATIVE	9	2	2	6	1	4
GOOD FUND-RAISER	0	1	0	3	4	2
HAS A GLOBAL VIEW	21	9	5	7	1	7
INTERNATIONALLY RESILIENT	3	1	1	2	0	1
LISTENS WELL	59	55	53	51	68	55
MENTORING	21	25	26	30	29	27
NUMERICALLY ASTUTE	12	7	9	6	3	7
OPTIMISTIC	26	25	22	28	45	28
PERCEPTIVE	35	30	33	35	16	31
PERSUASIVE	24	34	37	34	16	31
PHYSICALLY FIT	6	7	3	2	5	4
PUBLICLY IMPRESSIVE	15	8	9	14	11	11
RESOURCEFUL	24	32	21	26	14	24
SUPPORTIVE	9	17	17	16	39	19
SYSTEMATIC	18	17	19	13	8	15
TACTFUL	21	17	17	20	18	18
TRUSTED	59	61	60	58	56	59
TRUSTING	29	21	25	20	40	25
WELL CONNECTED	9	12	17	13	20	15
WHOLESOME	3	6	5	3	9	5

Note: The difference between two generations' responses is statistically significant (note for the statistically minded: "statistically significant" here is at the 99% confidence level or $p < 0.01$) if the difference between the two percentages is greater than the number that follows for each pair:

S = Silents; EB = Early Boomers; LB = Late Boomers; EX = Early Xers; LX = Late Xers

S – EB > 26%	EB – LB > 17%	LB – EX > 19% EX – LX > 18%
S – LB > 25%	EB – EX > 17%	LB – LX > 18%
S – EX > 25%	EB – LX > 16%	
S – LX > 27%		

For example, let's look at the data for DELEGATING:

	S	EB	LB	EX	LX
DELEGATING	50	30	29	23	10

We see that significantly more Early Boomers than Late Xers chose this attribute (30% versus 10%, with the difference of 20% being greater than the cut-off difference of 16%). However, the difference between Late Boomers and Early Xers (29% versus 23%, or a difference of 6%) is smaller than the cut-off difference of 19% and hence is not statistically significant.

$N = 544$ (34 Silents, 109 Early Boomers, 150 Late Boomers, 171 Early Xers, and 80 Late Xers)

Note: This list of attributes is adapted from the work of David Campbell and used with permission. An assessment instrument created from this material is also available: *Campbell Leadership Descriptor,* San Francisco: Pfeiffer, 2002.

Percentage of Respondents Who Placed Each Leadership Attribute in Their Top Three, by Generation

LEADERSHIP ATTRIBUTE	Silents (%)	Early Boomers (%)	Late Boomers (%)	Early Xers (%)	Late Xers (%)	Overall (%)
A GOOD COACH	6	6	5	9	6	7
A GOOD TEACHER	9	4	5	5	6	5
ADVENTURESOME	6	3	2	2	0	2
BALANCED	6	4	4	9	3	5
CANDID AND HONEST	15	8	12	10	3	9
CREATIVE	18	8	7	5	9	8
CREDIBLE	32	33	43	29	19	32
CULTURALLY SENSITIVE LEADER	6	6	3	2	1	3
DEDICATED	9	5	11	8	26	11
DELEGATING	0	2	5	4	3	3
DEPENDABLE	18	17	20	20	26	20
DIPLOMATIC	3	6	6	7	1	5
DURABLE	3	3	1	3	3	2
ENCOURAGING	3	10	11	5	11	9

LEADERSHIP ATTRIBUTE	Silents (%)	Early Boomers (%)	Late Boomers (%)	Early Xers (%)	Late Xers (%)	Overall (%)
ENERGETIC	9	3	1	4	8	4
ENTERPRISING	3	3	4	5	1	3
EXPERIENCED	21	11	20	15	19	17
FARSIGHTED	32	29	37	35	13	31
FOCUSED	9	13	9	8	20	11
GLOBAL LEADERSHIP IMAGE	0	1	1	2	0	1
GLOBALLY INNOVATIVE	3	0	1	1	1	1
GOOD FUND-RAISER	0	1	0	0	0	0
HAS A GLOBAL VIEW	9	4	1	5	0	3
INTERNATIONALLY RESILIENT	0	1	0	0	0	0
LISTENS WELL	12	23	13	16	19	17
MENTORING	9	3	4	6	4	5
NUMERICALLY ASTUTE	3	0	2	0	0	1
OPTIMISTIC	0	6	2	9	18	7
PERCEPTIVE	6	9	9	11	3	9
PERSUASIVE	9	10	7	2	4	6
PHYSICALLY FIT	0	1	0	1	0	0
PUBLICLY IMPRESSIVE	0	1	1	2	3	2
RESOURCEFUL	0	7	3	5	1	4
SUPPORTIVE	0	4	2	5	13	5
SYSTEMATIC	3	2	3	4	3	3
TACTFUL	3	1	1	3	3	2
TRUSTED	24	39	32	29	26	31
TRUSTING	12	10	9	10	20	11
WELL CONNECTED	3	4	3	2	6	3
WHOLESOME	0	3	1	1	3	2

Note: The difference between two generations' responses is statistically significant (note for the statistically minded: "statistically significant" here is at the 99% confidence level or $p < 0.01$) if the difference between the two percentages is greater than the number that follows for each pair:

S = Silents; EB = Early Boomers; LB = Late Boomers; EX = Early Xers; LX = Late Xers

S – EB > 26%   EB – LB > 17%   LB – EX > 19%   EX – LX > 18%
S – LB > 25%   EB – EX > 17%   LB – LX > 18%
S – EX > 25%   EB – LX > 16%
S – LX > 27%

For example, let's look at the data for FARSIGHTED:

	S	EB	LB	EX	LX
FARSIGHTED	32	29	37	35	13

We see that significantly more Late Boomers than Late Xerss chose this attribute (37% versus 13%, with the difference of 24% being greater than the cut-off difference of 18%). However, the difference between Silents and Late Boomers (32% versus 37%, or a difference of 5%) is smaller than the cut-off difference of 25% and hence is not statistically significant.

$N = 544$ (34 Silents, 109 Early Boomers, 150 Late Boomers, 171 Early Xers, and 80 Late Xers)

Note: This list of attributes is adapted from the work of David Campbell and used with permission. An assessment instrument created from this material is also available: *Campbell Leadership Descriptor,* San Francisco: Pfeiffer, 2002.

Percentage of Respondents Who Placed Each Leadership Attribute in Their Top Ten, by Organizational Level

LEADERSHIP ATTRIBUTE	Top and Executive (%)	Upper Management (%)	Management (%)	Professional (%)
A GOOD COACH	39	39	41	40
A GOOD TEACHER	22	22	36	30
ADVENTURESOME	13	9	12	20
BALANCED	25	20	26	28
CANDID AND HONEST	30	31	33	21
CREATIVE	29	25	26	30
CREDIBLE	68	74	75	77
CULTURALLY SENSITIVE LEADER	8	7	11	16
DEDICATED	44	36	39	21
DELEGATING	22	31	30	26
DEPENDABLE	36	46	51	43
DIPLOMATIC	30	28	24	27
DURABLE	25	19	16	14
ENCOURAGING	42	48	51	48
ENERGETIC	17	16	16	13

LEADERSHIP ATTRIBUTE	Top and Executive (%)	Upper Management (%)	Management (%)	Professional (%)
ENTERPRISING	17	13	11	10
EXPERIENCED	30	41	35	37
FARSIGHTED	66	58	48	57
FOCUSED	51	38	42	43
GLOBAL LEADERSHIP IMAGE	4	3	1	5
GLOBALLY INNOVATIVE	3	5	4	7
GOOD FUND-RAISER	0	0	1	2
HAS A GLOBAL VIEW	10	8	4	12
INTERNATIONALLY RESILIENT	1	2	1	2
LISTENS WELL	53	48	51	58
MENTORING	23	27	26	27
NUMERICALLY ASTUTE	12	9	7	7
OPTIMISTIC	29	23	26	23
PERCEPTIVE	32	34	26	42
PERSUASIVE	45	37	30	30
PHYSICALLY FIT	5	6	4	1
PUBLICLY IMPRESSIVE	13	13	6	12
RESOURCEFUL	26	31	27	18
SUPPORTIVE	10	17	20	15
SYSTEMATIC	16	20	16	16
TACTFUL	13	20	21	22
TRUSTED	58	55	61	57
TRUSTING	10	21	26	29
WELL CONNECTED	19	14	11	14
WHOLESOME	4	4	6	2

Note: The difference between two levels' responses is statistically significant (note for the statistically minded: "statistically significant" here is at the 99% confidence level or $p < 0.01$) if the difference between the two percentages is greater than the number that follows for each pair:

T/EX = Top and Executive; UM = Upper Management;
M = Management; P = Professional

T/EX – UM > 20%   UM – M > 17%   M – P > 16%
T/EX – M > 19%   UM – P > 18%
T/EX – P > 19%

For example, let's look at the data for TRUSTING:

	T/EX	UM	M	P
TRUSTING	10	21	26	29

We see that significantly more Professionals than Top Executives chose this attribute (29% versus 10%, with the difference of 19% being exactly the cut-off difference). However, the difference between Professionals and Management (29% versus 26%, or a difference of 3%) is smaller than the cut-off difference of 16% and hence is not statistically significant.

$N = 440$ (77 Top and Executive, 108 Upper Management, 140 Management, 115 Professional)

Note: This list of attributes is adapted from the work of David Campbell and used with permission. An assessment instrument created from this material is also available: *Campbell Leadership Descriptor,* San Francisco: Pfeiffer, 2002.

Average Number of Jobs Worked During Each Age Period

	Silents (n = 192)	Early Boomers (n = 769)	Late Boomers (n = 808)	Early Xers (n = 854)	Late Xers (n = 120)
Current Age Range	60–80	51–59	42–50	29–41	18–28
Age	Average Number of Jobs	Average Number of Jobs	Average Number of Jobs	Average Number of Jobs	Average Number of Jobs
20–25	1.55	1.79	1.60	2.07	1.77
26–30	.99	1.11	.96	1.13	.19
31–35	.71	.72	.57	.58	
36–40	.59	.60	.50	.18	
41–45	.46	.42	.35		
46–50	.49	.42	.18		
51–55	.37	.32			

References and Suggested Reading

Preface

Dalton, M., Ernst, C., Deal, J., and Leslie, J. *Success for the New Global Manager: What You Need to Know to Work Across Distances, Countries, and Cultures.* San Francisco: Jossey-Bass, 2002.

Introduction

Dohm, A. "Gauging the Labor Force Effects of Retiring Baby-Boomers." *Monthly Labor Review,* 2000, *123*(7), 17–25.

Toosi, M. "Labor Force Projections to 2014: Retiring Boomers." *Monthly Labor Review,* 2005, *128*(11), 25–44.

Principle 1

Lencioni, P. M. "Make Your Values Mean Something." *Harvard Business Review,* 2002, *80*(7), 113–117.

Nash, L., and Stevenson, H. "Success That Lasts." *Harvard Business Review,* 2004, *82*(2), 102–109.

Sull, D., and Houlder, D. "Do Your Commitments Match Your Convictions?" *Harvard Business Review,* 2005, *83*(1), 82–91.

Principle 2

"In Praise of Boundaries." *Harvard Business Review,* 2003, *81*(12), 41–45.

Lawler, E. E., III. *Treat People Right! How Organizations and Individuals Can Propel Each Other into a Virtuous Spiral of Success.* San Francisco: Jossey-Bass, 2003.

Principle 3

Buckingham, M., and Coffman, C. *First, Break All the Rules: What the World's Greatest Managers Do Differently.* New York: Simon & Schuster, 1999.

Galford, R., and Drapeau, A. S. "The Enemies of Trust." *Harvard Business Review,* 2003, *81*(2), 88–95.

Galford, R. M., and Drapeau, A. S. *The Trusted Leader: Bringing Out the Best in Your People and Your Company.* New York: Free Press, 2002.

Graham, G. L. "If You Want Honesty, Break Some Rules." *Harvard Business Review,* 2002, *80*(4), 42–47.

Joni, S. A. "The Geography of Trust." *Harvard Business Review,* 2004, *82*(3), 82–88.

Kellaway, L. "Lucy Kellaway on Work: The Jack and Suzy Column Is Built on Shaky Foundations." *Financial Times,* October 24, 2005, 13.

Kramer, R. "Trust and Distrust in Organizations: Emerging Perspectives, Enduring Questions." *Annual Review of Psychology,* 1999, *50*(1), 569–598.

Prusak, L. "How to Invest in Social Capital." *Harvard Business Review,* 2001, *79*(6), 86–93.

Simons, T. "The High Cost of Lost Trust." *Harvard Business Review,* 2002, *80*(9), 18–19.

Young, L., and Daniel, K. "Affectual Trust in the Workplace." *International Journal of Human Resource Management,* 2003, *14*(1), 139–155.

Principle 4

Collins, J. *Good to Great.* New York: HarperCollins, 2001.

Graham, G. L. "If You Want Honesty, Break Some Rules." *Harvard Business Review,* 2002, *80*(4), 42–47.

Kellerman, B. "When Should a Leader Apologize and When Not?" *Harvard Business Review,* 2006, *84*(4), 72–81.

Lee, R. J., and King, S. N. *Discovering the Leader in You: A Guide to Realizing Your Personal Leadership Potential.* San Francisco: Jossey-Bass, 2001.

Loehr, J., and Schwartz, T. "The Making of a Corporate Athlete." *Harvard Business Review,* 2001, *79*(1), 120–128.

McDowell-Larsen, S. L., Campbell, D., and Kearney, L. "Fitness and Leadership: Is There a Relationship?" *Journal of Managerial Psychology,* 2002, *17*(4), 316–324.

Principle 5

Ciampa, D. "Almost Ready: How Leaders Move Up." *Harvard Business Review,* 2005, *83*(1), 46–53.

Frankel, L. P. *Nice Girls Don't Get the Corner Office: 101 Unconscious Mistakes Women Make That Sabotage Their Careers.* New York: Warner Business Books, 2004.

Gabarro, J. J., and Kotter, J. P. "Managing Your Boss." *Harvard Business Review,* 2005, *83*(1), 92–99.

Kramer, R. M. "When Paranoia Makes Sense." *Harvard Business Review,* 2002, *80*(7), 62–69.

Lakoff, G. *Moral Politics*. Chicago: University of Chicago Press, 1996.

McClelland, D. C., and Burnham, D. H. "Power Is the Great Motivator." *Harvard Business Review*, 2003, *81*(1), 117–126.

Michaels, E., Handfield-Jones, H., and Axelrod, B. *The War for Talent*. Cambridge, Mass.: Harvard Business School Press, 2001.

Neilson, G. L., Pasternack, B. A., and Van Nuys, K. E. "The Passive-Aggressive Organization." *Harvard Business Review*, 2005, *83*(10), 82–92.

Peebles, M. E., and others. "Into the Fray." *Harvard Business Review*, 2005, *83*(1), 15–18.

Principle 6

Kotter, J. P., and others. *Harvard Business Review on Change*. (Harvard Business Review Paperback Series). Cambridge, Mass.: Harvard Business School Press, 1998.

Roberto, M. A., and Levesque, L. C. "The Art of Making Change Initiatives Stick." *MIT Sloan Management Review*, Summer 2005, pp. 53–60.

Sirkin, H. L., Keenan, P., and Jackson, A. "The Hard Side of Change Management." *Harvard Business Review*, 2005, *83*(10), 108–118.

Strebel, P. "Why Do Employees Resist Change?" *Harvard Business Review*, 1996, *74*(3), 86–92.

Principle 7

Craig, E., Kimberly, J., and Bouchikhi, H. "Can Loyalty Be Leased?" *Harvard Business Review*, 2002, *80*(9), 24.

Dohm, A. "Gauging the Labor Force Effects of Retiring Baby-Boomers." *Monthly Labor Review*, 2000, *123*(7), 17–25.

Lawler, E. E., III. *Treat People Right! How Organizations and Individuals Can Propel Each Other into a Virtuous Spiral of Success*. San Francisco: Jossey-Bass, 2003.

Reichheld, F. F. *The Loyalty Effect: The Hidden Force Behind Growth, Profits, and Lasting Value*. Cambridge, Mass.: Harvard Business School Press, 1996.

Reichheld, F. F. *Loyalty Rules! How Today's Leaders Build Lasting Relationships*. Cambridge, Mass.: Harvard Business School Press, 2001.

Toosi, M. "Labor Force Projections to 2014: Retiring Boomers." *Monthly Labor Review*, 2005, *128*(11), 25–44.

Principle 8

Dohm, A. "Gauging the Labor Force Effects of Retiring Baby-Boomers." *Monthly Labor Review*, 2000, *123*(7), 17–25.

Dychtwald, K., Erickson, T., and Morison, R. "It's Time to Retire Retirement." *Harvard Business Review*, 2004, *82*(3), 48–57.

Fishman, C. "The War for Talent." *Fast Company*, July 1998, 104.

Geissler, C., Herrmann, N., Bovbjerg, B. D., Martina, D., and Kamerick,

E. A. "The Cane Mutiny: Managing a Graying Workforce." *Harvard Business Review,* 2005, *83*(10), 31–42.

Hewlett, S. A., and Luce, C. B. "Off-Ramps and On-Ramps." *Harvard Business Review,* 2005, *83*(3), 43–54.

Michaels, E., Handfield-Jones, H., and Axelrod, B. *The War for Talent.* Cambridge, Mass.: Harvard Business School Press, 2001.

Morison, R., Erickson, T., and Dychtwald, K. "Managing Middlescence." *Harvard Business Review,* 2006, *84*(3), 78–86.

Toosi, M. (2005). "Labor Force Projections to 2014: Retiring Boomers." *Monthly Labor Review,* 2005, *128*(11), 25–44.

Principle 9

Dalton, M., Ernst, C., Deal, J., and Leslie, J. *Success for the New Global Manager: What You Need to Know to Work Across Distances, Countries, and Cultures.* San Francisco: Jossey-Bass, 2002.

Lombardo, M. M., and Eichinger, R. W. *Eighty-Eight Assignments for Development in Place.* Greensboro, N.C.: Center for Creative Leadership, 1989.

Lombardo, M. M., and Eichinger, R. W. *FYI For Your Improvement* (4th ed.). Minneapolis: Lominger Limited, 2004.

McCauley, C. D. *Developmental Assignments: Creating Learning Experiences Without Changing Jobs.* Greensboro, N.C.: Center for Creative Leadership, 2006.

McCauley, C. D., and Van Velsor, E. (eds.). *The Center for Creative Leadership Handbook of Leadership Development* (2nd ed.). San Francisco: Jossey-Bass, 2004.

Sessa, V. I., and London, M. *Continuous Learning in Organizations: Individual, Group, and Organizational Perspectives.* Mahwah, N.J.: Erlbaum, 2006.

Principle 10

Berglas, S. "The Very Real Dangers of Executive Coaching." *Harvard Business Review,* 2002, *80*(6), 86–93.

Goldsmith, M., and Lyons, L. S. (eds.). *Coaching for Leadership: The Practice of Leadership Coaching from the World's Greatest Coaches* (2nd ed.). San Francisco: Pfeiffer, 2005.

"Introduction." In S. Ting and P. Scisco (eds.), *The CCL Handbook of Coaching: A Guide for the Leader Coach.* San Francisco: Jossey-Bass, 2006.

Morgan, H., Harkins, P., and Goldsmith, M. *The Art and Practice of Leadership Coaching: 50 Top Executive Coaches Reveal Their Secrets.* Hoboken, N.J.: Wiley, 2004.

Acknowledgments

Ross De Pinto, with assistance by Rebecca Booth, built the Web site that gathered the data. In addition, Ross continually provided a sounding board and double-checked statistics and conclusions. Ellen Van Velsor acted as our project advocate. CCL's assessment services group, library, and information technology group provided support and technical assistance both to us and to research participants. Karen Bryson, Kristen Axman, Nancy Staley, David Baldwin, David Jacobsen, Heidi Gailor-Loflin, and Dana McDonald-Mann started the project. Kelly Bartlett and Karissa McKenna both worked on the project for years. Ellen Conley supported us brilliantly. David Altman was always there with encouragement when I needed it. Always. David Berke continuously encouraged me and made suggestions for improving the research, its application, and the book. Alissa Nadel was there to help at the last minute when something came up. Stephanie Trovas and Karen Bryson continue to work on the project, which means they are contributing to everything in one way or another.

Outside CCL, dozens of people provided support, suggestions, and critical analysis over the years the project has run. Maura Stevenson made herself available to comment on everything—items, conclusions, presentations. Valerie Sessa spent considerable time discussing statistics and conclusions with me to make sure that inferences I made were based on good, solid evidence.

Pete Scisco, Byron Schneider, and Kathe Sweeney read multiple drafts of this manuscript. Regina Maruca acted as the developmental editor, prodding me to add more where I was too brief. Michele Jones did an exceptional job of copyediting. Karen Mayworth and Joanne Ferguson plunged ahead as deadlines loomed and details swarmed. Ronson Kung, Melissa Gratias, Maxine Dalton, David Dickter, Kristen Boyle, Barbara Troupin, Kevin Liu,

Karen Jellison, Kirsten Poehlmann, Marian Ruderman, Patty Ohlott, and others already mentioned read individual chapters to make sure I was being accurate and clear in my explanations.

As I mentioned in the Preface, this book would not have been written without the support and assistance of everyone listed here. In addition to those mentioned, there are hundreds of others not listed (colleagues, family, and friends) who helped in smaller though no less important ways, and I am grateful to you all.

About the Author

Jennifer J. Deal is a research scientist at the Center for Creative Leadership (CCL) in San Diego, California. Her work focuses on the areas of global leadership and generational differences. She is the manager of CCL's World Leadership Survey and the Emerging Leaders research project. In 2002 she was a coauthor of the book *Success for the New Global Manager: How to Work Across Distances, Countries, and Cultures,* published by Jossey-Bass. She has published articles on generational issues, global management, executive selection, and women in management. An internationally recognized expert on generational differences, she has spoken on the topic on six continents (North and South America, Europe, Asia, Africa, and Australia), and she looks forward to speaking to Antarctic penguins about their generational issues in the near future. She holds a B.A. from Haverford College and a Ph.D. in industrial/organizational psychology from The Ohio State University.

Index

About the Center for Creative Leadership

The Center for Creative Leadership (CCL) is a nonprofit, educational institution with international reach. Since the Center's founding in 1970, its mission has been to advance the understanding, practice, and development of leadership for the benefit of society worldwide.

Devoted to leadership education and research, CCL works annually with more than two thousand organizations and twenty thousand individuals from the private, public, education, and nonprofit sectors. The Center's five campuses span three continents: Greensboro, North Carolina; Colorado Springs, Colorado; and San Diego, California, in North America; Brussels, Belgium, in Europe; and Singapore in Asia. In addition, sixteen Network Associates around the world offer selected CCL programs and assessments.

CCL draws strength from its nonprofit status and educational mission, which provide unusual flexibility in a world where quarterly profits often drive thinking and direction. It has the freedom to be objective, wary of short-term trends, and motivated foremost by its mission—hence our substantial and sustained investment in leadership research. Although CCL's work is always grounded in a strong foundation of research, it focuses on achieving a beneficial impact in the real world. Its efforts are geared to be practical and action oriented, helping leaders and their organizations more effectively achieve their goals and vision. The desire to transform learning and ideas into action provides the impetus for CCL's programs, assessments, publications, and services.

Capabilities

CCL's activities encompass leadership education, knowledge generation and dissemination, and building a community centered on leadership. CCL is broadly recognized for excellence in executive education, leadership development, and innovation by sources such as *BusinessWeek,* the *Financial Times,* the *New York Times,* and the *Wall Street Journal.*

Open-Enrollment Programs

Fourteen open-enrollment courses are designed for leaders at all levels, as well as people responsible for leadership development and training at their organizations. This portfolio offers distinct choices for participants seeking a particular learning environment or type of experience. Some programs are structured specifically around small group activities, discussion, and personal reflection, while others offer hands-on opportunities through business simulations, artistic exploration, team-building exercises, and new-skills practice. Many of these programs offer private one-on-one sessions with a feedback coach.

For a complete listing of programs, visit http://www.ccl.org/programs.

Customized Programs

CCL develops tailored educational solutions for more than one hundred client organizations around the world each year. Through this applied practice, CCL structures and delivers programs focused on specific leadership development needs within the context of defined organizational challenges, including innovation, the merging of cultures, and the development of a broader pool of leaders. The objective is to help organizations develop, within their own cultures, the leadership capacity they need to address challenges as they emerge.

Program details are available online at http://www.ccl.org/custom.

Coaching

CCL's suite of coaching services is designed to help leaders maintain a sustained focus and generate increased momentum toward achieving their goals. These coaching alternatives vary in depth and duration and serve a variety of needs, from helping an executive sort through career and life issues to working with an organization to integrate coaching into its internal development process. Our coaching offerings, which can supplement program attendance or be customized for specific individual or team needs, are based on our ACS model of assessment, challenge, and support.

Learn more about CCL's coaching services at http://www.ccl.org/coaching.

Assessment and Development Resources

CCL pioneered 360-degree feedback and believes that assessment provides a solid foundation for learning, growth, and transformation and that development truly happens when an individual recognizes the need to change. CCL offers a broad selection of assessment tools, online resources, and simulations that can help individuals, teams, and organizations increase their self-awareness, facilitate their own learning, enable their development, and enhance their effectiveness.

CCL's assessments are profiled at http://www.ccl.org/assessments.

Publications

The theoretical foundation for many of our programs, as well as the results of CCL's extensive and often groundbreaking research, can be found in the scores of publications issued by CCL Press and through the Center's alliance with Jossey-Bass, a Wiley imprint. Among these are landmark works, such as *Breaking the Glass Ceiling, The Lessons of Experience,* and *The Center for Creative Leadership Handbook of Leadership Development,* as well as quick-read guidebooks focused on core aspects of leadership. CCL publications provide insights and practical advice to help individuals become more effective leaders, develop leadership training within organizations, address issues of change and diversity, and build the systems and strategies that advance leadership collectively at the institutional level.

A complete listing of CCL publications is available at http://www.ccl. org/publications.

Leadership Community

To ensure that the Center's work remains focused, relevant, and important to the individuals and organizations it serves, CCL maintains a host of networks, councils, and learning and virtual communities that bring together alumni, donors, faculty, practicing leaders, and thought leaders from around the globe. CCL also forges relationships and alliances with individuals, organizations, and associations that share its values and mission. The energy, insights, and support from these relationships help shape and sustain CCL's educational and research practices and provide its clients with an added measure of motivation and inspiration as they continue their lifelong commitment to leadership and learning.

To learn more, visit http://www.ccl.org/connected.

Research

CCL's portfolio of programs, products, and services is built on a solid foundation of behavioral science research. The role of research at CCL is to advance the understanding of leadership and to transform learning into practical tools for participants and clients. CCL's research is the hub of a cycle that transforms knowledge into applications and applications into knowledge, thereby illuminating the way organizations think about and enact leadership and leader development.

Find out more about current research initiatives at http://www.ccl.org/research.

For additional information about CCL, please visit http://www.ccl.org or call Client Services at 336-545-2810.